Fire & Water Cooking

The Fusion of Smoking, Grilling, and Sous Vide Cooking Methods to make Amazing Food

By Darrin Wilson

Copyright © 2020 Fire and Water Cooking LLC.
All rights reserved. No part of this book may be used or reproduced without written permission unless it is part of another copy written book or website who has given you permission.
Published by
Fire and Water Cooking LLC
4463 Stoney River Dr
Mulberry, FL 33860
ISBN: 978-1-7358571-0-7

DEDICATION

This book is dedicated to my wife Lola, and kids Kraig, Spencer, and Rachel who have all suffered through my many experiments, hours of studying and tweaking, my many different grills and equipment testing, and for being my guinea pigs on recipes and all other research I have done to make this book possible. My brother in law, Keith Raygor, also helped me a ton with this book and many other things with this work. I could not have done it without all of your love and full support! Love you all so much!

TABLE OF CONTENTS

	About this book	Pg. 1
1	Cooking with Fire	Pg. 3
2	Cooking with Water	Pg. 10
3	Why Combine the Methods?	Pg. 19
4	Grills, Smokers, and Other Outdoor Cookers	Pg. 23
5	Sous Vide Equipment and Accessories	Pg. 29
6	Hot & Fast Cooking Tips & Techniques	Pg. 35
7	Low & Slow Cooking Tips & Techniques	Pg. 39
8	Converting Traditional Recipes	Pg. 43
9	Basic Recipes and Techniques	Pg. 47
	a) Appetizers & Finger Foods	Pg. 49
	b) Beef (Roasts, Steaks Burgers, and More)	Pg. 56
	c) Lamb (Roasts, Ribs, Chops, and More)	Pg. 69
	d) Pork (Ribs, Roasts, Pig Wings, and More)	Pg. 76
	e) Poultry (Chicken, Turkey, Duck, and More)	Pg. 85
	f) Seafood (Fish, Shrimp, Scallops, and More)	Pg. 94
	g) Vegetable Based (Tofu, Cauliflower, Portobello)	Pg. 100
10	Time and Temperature Information and References	Pg. 106
	Recipe Index	Pg. 112
	About the Author	Pg. 113

Fire & Water Cooking

ACKNOWLEDGMENTS

I would like to thank and acknowledge the many people who helped teach me, inspired me, and supported me along my path in creating the Fire & Water Cooking brand! These are just a few, but some of the most influential to me!

>Jason Logsdon of Amazing Food Made Easy
>Mike LaCharite of the International Sous Vide Association
>Kevin Liddell of Sous Vide Food and Fun
>Lloyd Cupiccia of "The Kosher Dosher" Food Blog
>Meathead Goldwyn of Amazingribs.com
>John Setzler of Man Cave Meals
>Greg Mrvich of Ballistic BBQ
>J. Kenji Lopez-Alt of "The Food Lab"

Please check out "The International Sous Vide Association" which is a group of many professional sous vide chefs, industry experts, and just plain food geeks who love to learn and teach about the ever expanding uses of the sous vide cooking method! They also hold the annual "Sous Vide Summit" which offers many presentations, classes, demonstrations, and much more! www.Theisva.org

You can also check out the book "Champions of Sous vide" on Amazon where you will find recipes from the top sous vide professionals in the world including two from yours truly! https://amzn.to/3iLPuc4

ABOUT THIS BOOK

First of all, I want you to know this is not really so much of a recipe book, but more of a Technique and How To book with a few recipes to demonstrate those techniques. I operate under the assumption that all cooking methods are NOT at war with each other or competing for our attention in the indoor or outdoor kitchens. I look at cooking methods like I do appliances and gadgets, as tools to be used to help create fantastic food to feed ourselves and our loved ones. In all cooking (and eating) you will have personal tastes and personal preferences in how you cook, how you season, and what tools you find more helpful than others.

You will not find recipes here for egg bites or other fancy dishes as I want to focus on the more traditional barbecue proteins here and the processes that work best for them. There are many other books available that address all that sous vide can do, but this is a book dedicated to sous vide and barbecue! No fancy plates, no pretty pictures, no desserts, just good food. I have included a few "Vegetable based" recipes also for those on a meatless diet.

I'm always open to new ideas and trying new methods while looking at why they work. In barbecue and cooking in general, there have always been those who try to tell you "this is how you must cook that" or "you need to follow this recipe exactly", pretty much they want you to cook exactly like they do. That's not me and I always suggest people try things multiple ways and find out how they or their family like the results. I am all for people giving suggestions and even giving legitimate reasons for why some things work better than others for them, but to assign a Right or Wrong way to something as subjective as cooking and personal taste is just not me.

This book is designed to introduce you to different methods and techniques that I have found to work well when incorporating sous vide with outdoor cooking along with some of the reasons why they work. These are things I've found to work for me.

Look at this book as a way to learn and try some new methods and processes that may make your cooking easier and possibly more enjoyable. Sous Vide will not replace smoking or grilling or any other cooking method, but it can be used like any other tool to create things that were not possible without it! So, now let's go play with our food!

PARTNERS, PRODUCTS, AND RECOMMENDATIONS

Over the years I have tested and tried many different products and have partnered with a few different companies. I am very particular with what I use as I look for products to give an overall value to me and the people that follow me. I do a lot of research, studying, and trial before I put my stamp of approval on any product. I have seen many other YouTubers and "Influencers" give glowing reviews on just pure junk in order to get free products or money. Some of them have new grills or smokers just about every month and sometimes don't give honest reviews! Well, that is not me. I use all the products I recommend, and if they don't meet my standards, I toss them. I like to partner with high quality companies and stick with them as much as possible. Below is a list of some of my favorite brands and partners.

Kamado Joe Ceramic Grills - Hasty Bake Charcoal Grills - Traeger Pellet Grills Anova Culinary - Inkbird Products - Camp Chef - Fogo Charcoal - The MeatStick Wireless Thermometers - Avid Armor and JVR Industries vacuum sealers

You can find most of the products I endorse or use in my Amazon Store located here - https://www.amazon.com/shop/fireandwatercooking and you can also find recommended reading and reviews on my main website under the "Recommend" page here – www.fireandwatercooking.com/fireandwaterrecommendedproducts

I use FreshJax Organic Seasonings for all my recipes, and I am proud to be partnering with them on this book. They offer the freshest all-natural ingredients with no additives or anti-caking agents, many great seasoning blends, spices, and herbs. You can find them on their website here: http://freshjax.refr.cc/darrin

Disclosure
We do participate in affiliate marketing campaigns that compensate us for sales generated through these links at no added cost to you, to help us create more content and pay the bills. Thanks for supporting us and our sponsors!

Fire & Water Cooking

CHAPTER 1
COOKING WITH FIRE

Man has been cooking with fire long before the internet even existed, LOL. Nothing gets me more excited than the smell of charcoal and burning wood in my smoker ready for me to toss a hunk of meat on it for dinner with friends and family! Some of my fondest memories as a child are of attending the local festival in town where they would have Cornel BBQ Chicken cooking over a charcoal fire pit and served with all the sides.

Even though we have been cooking over fire forever, there are still many new and exciting products and technology coming out on a regular basis to get more people excited about cooking outside. There are many super talented people out there teaching and preaching the gospel of cooking over live fire and smoke for sure. Since I started the Fire & Water Cooking Podcast in 2019, I have had many great barbecue celebrities and experts on the show such as Meathead Goldwyn of AmazingRibs.com, Malcolm Reed of "How to BBQ Right", Barbecue Legend Steven Raichlen, Danielle "Diva Q" Bennett, Susie Bullock of "Hey Grill Hey", and many more. While there is still a lot of tradition and history in barbecue and outdoor cooking, there is still room for new and exciting things that can be cooked outside with fire and smoke! This book will help expand your options.

In the last ten years or so, technology has inserted itself into the outdoor cooking space Big Time! With the invention of the pellet grill, smoker pit temperature controllers, Wi-Fi and Bluetooth controlled charcoal grills, flat top griddles, and tons of other accessories and tools, it's much easier for the regular guy to become a pitmaster. We've come a long way from the basic kettle grill cooking burgers and hot dogs, for sure.

That is why it was just natural for me to experiment with mixing the cooking methods of barbecue and grilling with sous vide. I have always considered "smoke" as just another seasoning for food, just like salt and pepper and I always consider what the flavor profiles are of the different types of smoking wood I am using to make sure it pairs well with what I happen to be cooking. So, since smoke can be considered just another seasoning option, let's dive in a little to how we can incorporate it.

First, let's talk a bit about the different types of outdoor cooking and just what they accomplish so we can see how sous vide can work with them.

Grilling and Searing

This is what everyone grew up with - either a charcoal grill or a gas grill cooking stuff hot and fast like burgers, hot dogs, chicken, sausages, and even the occasional steak. I can still smell the lighter fluid in the air at the local park from all of the families celebrating summertime. This type of cooking is pretty easy, what you want to do is make sure it's done, but not burned to death. Using a really hot fire, you quickly flip the meat before it catches on fire. In the last few years, Flat Top grills (Griddles) from companies such as Blackstone, Camp Chef, and others have exploded on the scene and many people are using them to cook a variety of things on them like stir-fries, smash burgers, breakfast, and much more. Back when I was growing up, we had no idea what an "Instant Read" thermometer was, so we could not measure the internal temperature of the meat. You either guessed or cut the meat open a little to make sure it was done.

But today we have many different tools to tell us if the food is cooked to the perfect temperature. Grilling and searing give the food we cook a nice crust, or char, also known as the "Maillard Reaction". This is what makes smash burgers and steaks taste so good. Sure, you can sear meat inside on a stove top in a pan, but on a grill, you have the chance to incorporate some smoke to it, either just from the charcoal or with a little wood added to the fire. Grilling can be done with either direct heat (over open flame or coals) or indirect heat (meat is not over the flame).

You can even use both direct and indirect together to do something called reverse sear or a pre-sear cook. A reverse sear cook is where you cook the meat on the indirect heat for the first part of the cook until it reaches a certain internal temperature, let's say 126f/53c for medium rare, and then you Sear it over an open flame at a much hotter temperature to get the Maillard Reaction crust. The pre-sear method works the other way, you sear the meat first to get the crust, then finish it on the indirect heat until it hits the desired doneness.

In both of these cooks you would experience some carry over cooking (more on that later in this section), which means the internal temperature continues to rise after you remove it from the heat. This is why you would remove the meat when it hits a temperature a few degrees below your desired doneness. For example, if you want medium-rare (132F/55c) removing the meat when it hits 126F/53c gives you some room for carry over cooking. Carry over cooking is one of the things that using the sous vide method helps you avoid when searing and grilling.

Baking, Roasting, and Braising

Believe it or not, you can roast and braise on a modern grill pretty easy now. Pellet grills, ceramic Kamado grills, and even kettle grills either have built in racks or accessories that make these cooking methods possible. Just because you cook on a smoker does not mean everything has to be smoked. Usually charcoal does not impart a big smoke flavor to food so it can be used to bake or roast just about anything! Bread, pizza, lasagna, meatloaf, pretty much anything you can cook in an indoor oven can be cooked on these grills/smokers. But the main thing all of these cookers have in common is **they all cook with heated air, and air is not the most efficient way to transfer heat to a protein**. Typically, the words Baking, and Roasting are used interchangeably. Baking is usually done at temperatures under 375f/190c and Roasting is commonly considered at higher temps that produce more of the browning "Maillard Reaction" we discussed earlier. Although braising involves liquid to cook, the liquid is still using air to heat it up and you really have no way to control the exact temperature of the liquid you are cooking with.

With a lot of cooks using baking, roasting, and braising, you not only cook the protein, but you are breaking down collagen and connective tissue that make the meat tough and render fat. Even within these cooking methods you can do either "Hot and Fast" or "Low and Slow" where you cook with lower or higher temperatures with shorter or longer cook times. Both of these methods produce different results. Since "smoking" things like brisket and pork butt are still technically roasting, I will discuss this in more detail in the following sections.

Hot and Fast Cooking

It used to be "Hot and Fast" meant grilling and searing like discussed in the previous section. But now it also can refer to some more traditionally low and slow type cooks using a slightly higher temperature to get similar results in a shorter time. Just like the term implies, it is referring to a higher temperature and shorter cooking time then low and slow. To give you some examples of a "hot and fast" cook when grilling, it would mean cooking a steak over an open flame, as close to the fire as possible, trying to get the crust built and the internal temperature as close to done as possible in very little time.

One technique people use for this is called "Just Keep Flipping" where they flip the steak every 10 seconds or so as to not let the surface burn and overcook the interior. In those instances, you are usually dealing with an already tender piece of meat, so you are not looking for the cook to help you make it more tender like you are in a usual "low and slow" cook. But it can also refer to someone who cooks a brisket or pork butt at a higher temperature than the normal range of 225f/107c-275f/135c in traditional cooks. Even though they are still cooking more "low and slow" compared to grilling or searing, compared to the normal/traditional cooking method they are using "hot and fast".

When cooking tough cuts of meat like brisket, pork butt, ribs, etc. you are using the temperature and time to not just cook, but to break down connective tissue, collagen, and render fat. An example of a "Hot and Fast" barbecue cook: the pit master would be cooking a brisket at around 400f/204c for the first part of the cook to get the bark set with a good Maillard Reaction and/or until it gets close to the normal barbecue stall internal temperature of 160f/71c. (The barbecue stall is when the internal temperature of the meat seems to get stuck without rising for a long period of time due to evaporative cooling.) Then they wrap it in either foil or butcher paper and lower the temperature back down to around 275f/135c to allow it to break down to tenderize and render fat. This allows them to finish a cook that would normally take 10-12 hours or more in half the time.

As with any cooking method, hot and fast has its ups and downs. Unless you are using a really well-marbled piece of meat with a lot of fat to render, it can dry it out and produce a sub-par end result. Cooking at hotter temperatures makes the meat proteins constrict more and push out a lot more moisture than if you cooked it lower. Not only that, the higher temperature will cause faster evaporation as well, meaning moisture leaves the meat at a much faster rate. You will not see many pitmasters doing "Hot and Fast" brisket cooking on anything under a Prime graded or Wagyu packer brisket because the extra fat will help keep it moist.

Low and Slow Cooking

Just like it reads, this method takes more time and uses lower temperatures. As I explained, larger and tougher cuts of meat need a lower temperature for a longer time to break down collagen, connective tissue, and to render larger pockets of fat in order for them to be delicious. This can be done in your oven as well as a grill or smoker, for sure. With the addition of smoke to the process you also get another flavor profile that a lot of people love.

The extra time in the cooker using wood allows for the outside of the meat to develop a wonderful crust or "bark" that can make for some of the best eating in your life. This bark usually starts to be created early on in the cooking process when the cold, wet meat starts to attract and interact with the smoke particles in the air. Cold, wet meat acts like a magnet to smoke and the constant flow of hot air dries the moisture leaving behind the aforementioned bark. Pit masters like to occasionally add more moisture by "spritzing" the meat with more liquids, like water, apple juice, etc. to help attract more smoke and make the bark deeper and darker. You don't really need "smoke" to develop a nice bark, but it does add another seasoning aspect to whatever you are cooking low and slow. If you have watched any videos or TV shows such as BBQ PitMasters, you have no doubt seen people "wrap" their meats during the cook at some point.

Wrapping these tough meats helps concentrate the heat and moisture to help speed up the process of breaking down the connective tissue and collagen, which turns into gelatin usually when the internal temperature reaches a certain point over 200f/94c. This is also done after the "bark" is set and has very little chance that the moisture inside the wrapping will adversely affect it. Using foil or butcher paper is most common. Foil tends to trap more moisture and can give the meat a "pot roast" type texture, so it has become popular to use pink butcher paper as that tends to allow some of the moisture to escape, but not all.

One of the main drawbacks of using the conventional cooking methods with hot air, is that you must cook the meat past the well-done phase in order to make it tender. This is one of the major benefits of mixing the methods of sous vide with traditional cooking as ONLY by using sous vide can we make these types of meats tender AND Medium rare. We will cover more about that in chapter 3.

Other Cooking Methods and Types

As we continue to move more of our cooking outside, we have had a large growth of people building full "outdoor kitchens" that offer up more ways to cook. Every year you see more people doing "deep fried turkey", more and more grill companies are offering attachments and add-ons such as rotisseries, pizza cooking set-ups, gas and induction burners, making our backyards the place we want to cook! It seems like there is no end to the new and different products offered every year aimed at the back-yard home chef.

The great thing about all of these new toys is that they all aimed at getting people excited about cooking at home, entertaining, and making it easier and more fun. That is what this book is all about. I will be showing you in the later chapters of this book just how the cooking method of sous vide can *enhance* and be another tool in your quiver in your outdoor kitchen. Even if you have just a lowly kettle or gas burning grill you will still be able to use these techniques to create food you can't make any other way.

Carry Over Cooking

This happens in most traditional cooking methods that use heated air to cook as you are always cooking at a higher temperature than you want your finished product to be. The internal temperature of your meat will continue to rise for a time after it is removed from the heat due to thermodynamics. The length of time can be determined by the thickness and type of meat. It is much more noticeable in "Hot & Fast" cooking due to the much hotter cooking temperature, but you will get this in "Low & Slow" cooking also.

Resting Meat

Heating proteins at a rapid rate makes them contract and expel moisture and move it from the interior of the meat to the exterior of the meat. This is why you want to rest your meat or remove from the heat for a certain time before serving. That will give the internal temperature time to peak and start to reduce back down and relax the protein strands of the meat some, allowing more of the moisture to remain in your food. Using sous vide, you can avoid carry-over cooking on most all cooks due to cooking at an exact temperature the whole time.

Fire & Water Cooking

CHAPTER 2
COOKING WITH WATER (SOUS VIDE)

What is Sous Vide?

There are many other books on the market that go into the history and nature of sous vide cooking, but this book will focus on the basics and how you can incorporate it into outdoor cooking. The words "Sous Vide" are French for "Under Vacuum". That is in reference to the cooking vessel itself, the vacuum sealed bag or zipper bag that the food is placed in while it is cooking in a precise temperature-controlled water bath. Although the cooking method itself has been around since the 1970's, up until just a few years ago the technology and understanding of what it could do were relegated to being used in commercial applications or higher end restaurants. The cost of the water baths or commercial circulators that were originally used in a laboratory setting were expensive, not many people even took the time to even try to understand the process. If you are interested in learning more about the history of sous vide and the development of modern-day equipment, I urge you to visit the website for CREA (Culinary Resource and Education Academy www.leCrea.com) where the pioneer of the sous vide method, Dr. Bruno Goussault still teaches and researches this amazing and versatile cooking method today. Below is a listing of what Sous Vide is and what it is not.

What Sous Vide Is – A precise lower temperature cooking method that uses food in a plastic bag, a water bath and heating device to efficiently transfer heat into and cook food. Sous vide is the "Ultimate Low and Slow Cooking". It can also be done in a precise temperature steam or combi oven with a "Sous Vide" option.

What Sous Vide Is Not – Boiling food in a bag, as sous vide uses lower temperatures of between 128f/53c and 190f/87.77c. It is not just another kitchen gadget. It is not "Only Good for Steaks".

What Can Sous Vide Do?

Ok, so what makes sous vide so different from other cooking methods? Why does it even matter if it uses water instead of air to cook with? What can it do that my oven and other cooking methods can't? Sous Vide is one of those things that has a HUGE range of applications and we have really only just started scratching the surface.

The reason it has so many applications is due to the fact that you can get a precise temperature to cook your food in. Most people do not realize that your home ovens, grills, and smokers cook at very inconsistent temperatures. Even though you set your oven to 350F to cook your chicken, it can have swings from 300f to 385f and all points

Fire & Water Cooking

in-between during the whole cook time. This is mainly due to the fact that air is not the best conductor of heat.

One of the things we need to understand I first learned from my friend Meathead Goldwyn over at AmazingRibs.com. It is his description of the different types of "Energies" or heat we use to cook with. In his article "The Thermodynamics of Cooking" he explains the three ways energy is transferred to food during cooking. They are Convection, Radiant, and Conductive. To paraphrase his description of these, he uses an example of young lovers to demonstrate the differences: Convection = your lover blowing in your ear, Radiant = The heat you feel coming off your lovers body under the sheets without touching, Conductive = The heat you feel when your bodies are pressed together. Yeah, it is kind of silly, but it sure does paint a mental picture! He also likes to use this example of why "Conductive Heat" is more powerful than "Convection".

Using a relatively low temperature of let's say 225f/107c in your oven, you can stick your arm in it without touching the sides and you will not get burned by the convection "air". But grab the side of the oven wall and the conductive heat will have you heading to the hospital with third degree burns. So, lets learn of the things that sous vide can do.

- ❖ **The first thing sous vide can do: Transfer heat much more efficiently than other cooking methods.**

Sous vide uses Conductive heat. Since we are using a viscous liquid such as water to heat the food, we can control the cooking temperature much easier and use lower temperatures to arrive at the doneness levels we cannot do when we use the other heat transfer methods of radiation and convection. With those methods, we must cook at a hotter temperature than we want the product to finish at.

For example, say I want my ribeye steak to be cooked medium-rare at around 131f/55c using radiant heat on my cast iron pan. I have to get that pan much hotter than the 131f/55c I want the steak to finish at, usually around 4 times hotter. Meathead uses the example here of being on a train going 100mph and trying to jump off exactly at the station while it is moving. It is hard to do and is usually hard to nail it just right. But since sous vide we are cooking the steak at EXACTLY the temperature we want it cooked to, say 131f/55c, we end up with a perfectly cooked steak from end to end. Yes, I know we would still need to sear the steak to get it just right, but I will cover that later on in chapter three.

- ❖ **The second thing sous vide can do: Cook to the exact temperature.**

Another thing that makes sous vide stand out is you can cook for very long times at the exact temperature you want. Why does this matter? Well, the same reason we use the "low and slow" method in traditional cooking, sous vide is the "ultimate low and slow" as it can go lower and does not need a lot of attention when it is cooking since there is no fire to attend to. As long as you have power the circulator will keep on chugging along. The longer times allow the meat to tenderize and breakdown the collagen and connective tissue just like the low and slow barbecue.

Being able to cook to an exact temperature is not just beneficial to meats, it can work amazing wonders for vegetables, starches, and pretty much anything. Since you are cooking a bag, you also do not have the negative effects that boiling or steaming has on these types of foods. Water is a solvent, and when you boil food in it, it removes flavors, vitamins, minerals, and all the good stuff. Trying sous vide mashed potatoes for the first time will open your eyes for sure.

❖ **The third thing sous vide can do: Low temperature pasteurization.**
If you're asking, "Why is that important?". Well, let me tell you, if you have never had chicken cooked lower than 165f/74c because the USDA guidelines tell you that is where it is "safe to eat", you have not lived yet. Lol! Being able to safely pasteurize proteins at lower cooking temperatures using longer times is awesome for poultry, pork, lamb, and even ground meat. Want a medium-rare thick hamburger without the risk of salmonella? Sous vide is your ticket! Have you ever wondered what pork tenderloin tastes like cooked to 135f/57c? Now is your chance! And you don't need to figure out the pasteurization tables on your own, either.

Douglas Baldwin wrote the complete guide to safe times and temperatures a few years back and his website is easy to bookmark, and it is free. Check out his website and book "Sous Vide for the Home Cook". He has tons of information that is pretty easy to understand but is also very detailed. He also goes into why you also need to consider the thickness of your meats when trying to figure out the pasteurization times and temperatures.

❖ **The fourth thing sous vide can do: Produce moister meats.**
If we go back to the article on AmazingRibs.com "The Thermodynamics of Cooking" you will learn that meat is made up of about 75% water. When heat is applied to it you will start to have all kinds of reactions. Cooking starts to take place from the outside and moves inward. Since you are cooking at lower temperatures and you are cooking in a sealed bag, you will not have as much evaporation as you would if you were cooking in heated air. But you will still have moisture loss due to the muscle proteins contracting and squeezing out the excess liquid between them. Since you are cooking at lower

temperatures and staying there, the contractions will stop when it hits the cooking temp throughout the meat. You would lose much more moisture in a traditional cook due to the fact that you are cooking at higher temperatures and you have evaporation taking place. Another benefit for something like pulled pork or beef, you can add the remaining bag juices back into it to make it much moister and more flavorful. Recently there have been some studies by CREA and other sous vide experts into something called "Step Down Cooking" where they start the cook off at a higher temperature, then back it down to a lower temperature for a time, and it may show the possibility of some re-absorption of moisture. That is still being tested, but it does pose another possibility of sous vide producing much more moist meats than traditional cooks, but I will save that for another book.

❖ **The fifth thing sous vide can do: Speed up the brining process.**

One of the things we can do to meat to make sure it retains moisture no matter how we are cooking it, is by "brining" it with salt. This is usually done in two different ways. You can either soak the meat in a salted water which is known as "wet brining" or you can "dry brine" by adding salt to the exterior of the meat and let it sit in the refrigerator for a certain time. Salt is the only seasoning that will penetrate the surface of the meat, and it allows it to retain moisture in the cells. When you cook at low temperatures, the heat will speed up the brining process letting the salt penetrate deeper and faster than just sitting in the fridge. To learn more about brining, including how low temperature cooking speeds up the process, you need to read this article on AmazingRibs.com ["Salting and Wet Brining"](#).

❖ **The sixth thing sous vide can do: Tenderize tough meats at a much lower temperature.**

This is what got me excited the most about sous vide when I first started researching it. Coming from a low and slow barbecue background, I know that you really need lower temperatures and longer times to break down the tough meats in order to make them edible. Going too hot will dry it out and burn it up and not produce anything you would brag about for sure. To try and get a brisket or beef ribs tender traditionally, you have to get them up over 200F/94c internal temperature, so the collagen and connective tissue breaks down into gelatin. But, with sous vide you don't have to get the internal temperature that high. By using longer times at exact, lower temperatures, sous vide allows you to make things like a tender juicy brisket medium-rare! Beefy, unctuous beef short ribs can also be done at medium-rare to medium doneness. Some of the first cooks I did mixing sous vide, and barbecue are these types of cooks. We will explore this much deeper later in this book.

Sous vide can do much more than these few things I have pointed out, but we are going to stick with these for now because of how it can be used in relation to smoke and grilling.

What Equipment is used in Sous Vide Cooking?

Now that I got your interest peaked, let's talk a little about the equipment. I will go deeper into this subject later in the book, but for right now we will talk in generalities.

Over the last several years, just like what has happened with outdoor cooking equipment and accessories, the cost of sous vide equipment has dropped, while the options have increased. With that being said, here is a short list of what you need to start with sous vide:

- **A Sous Vide circulator** – These can be had for anywhere from $40-$200 or more depending on the options you choose. These gadgets attach to the sides of a container filled with water and have built in heaters and fans that circulate the water to keep it at the exact temperature you choose. They also have timers that can notify you when the food is ready. I will address all the different options in another chapter dedicated to sous vide equipment.

- **Some kind of container to hold the water and food** – You can pretty much use any kind of container as long as it is sturdy enough and won't leak during the cook. For longer cooking times you will want some kind of cover to avoid excessive evaporation which can damage your circulator and have adverse effects on the food. People have used large stock pots, food storage containers, and even coolers that they have drilled a hole in the lid to accommodate the circulator.

- **Vacuum sealer or other food storage bags** - You do not *have* to use a vacuum sealer, but it makes life easier and can be used for much more than sous vide. Any kind of food safe storage bag will work as well, and you can use the "Water Displacement" method where you load the food into the bag and slowly insert the bag into the water. The water will remove the air from the bag, and you can either close the bag or clip it to the side of the container during the cook. For larger meats I highly recommend using a vacuum sealer and expandable bags. More on that later in Chapter 5.

- **An accurate time and temperature guide** - To make sure you are using safe and tried and true times and temperatures; I highly recommend you use a guide that gives you ranges instead of set times and temperatures to give you a better chance for success. One of my favorite sources is my friend Jason Logsdon's website here: www.amazingfoodmadeeasy.com

- **A way to sear or finish the meat** - You'll want to be ready beforehand for which method you'll use to get a good sear or bark, by using your pan, torch, grill, smoker or another method.

- **A good instant read thermometer** - these are so helpful when you are wanting to make sure you do not overcook your meat. You can get them so cheap now that it makes sense to always have one on hand.

That is pretty much it. Later in the book we'll dive deeper into what other equipment and accessories are available and what they can help you with.

Sous Vide Basics

Now let's discuss some basic things you need to know about sous vide that you may not be familiar with. These are some good guidelines to help you better understand some of the "why's" and "how's". Below are some subjects that come up in the online sous vide groups often so I thought I would address them here.

- **Don't cook too Low for too Long -** Some people like their steaks rare, or even "Blue" which is mostly raw. Where rare is attainable, there is really not much of a benefit that sous vide can offer when cooking temperatures are below 128f/53.33c, and they can actually be unsafe if cooked for a longer time in the sous vide. You can't do much tenderizing or pasteurizing at those lower temperatures so I would avoid them altogether. If you like rare or blue steaks, stick to conventional hot and fast searing.

- **Don't cook for really long times on tender meat -** if the meat is already tender, like a filet for instance, going for a longer time than necessary can make it mushy and completely ruin the texture. This can also happen on more tough proteins, so just try to stay within proven and posted time ranges for the doneness level you are looking for.

- **Know when and why to ice bath -** There are a couple different reasons to use an ice bath to drop the internal temperature of your food after sous vide cooking. One is to make sure you do not "overcook" the meat during the searing or smoking process. I suggest you do this with thinner steaks and chops, and most things you will be smoking for a longer time. Use an instant read thermometer to monitor your food during the sear or smoking to make sure you do not overcook.

  The second reason to ice bath is for food safety reasons if you will be storing the food after sous vide to finish later. Even though your food may be pasteurized and in a sealed bag, there are still some pathogens that can survive and grow if the food sits in the "Danger Zone" too long. So, I highly suggest if you are going to pre-cook and finish later, ice bath the food before storing in the refrigerator.

- **The proper way to sear -** When searing a steak, roast, or any other meat, you need to make sure you pat them dry as much as possible. It takes a lot more energy to evaporate water than it does to produce a great sear, so the less moisture on the surface, the better. Also, when using such seasonings as dried herbs and pepper, be aware it can burn and leave a bitter taste on the meat if using a torch.

- **Do Not add butter, oil, fresh herbs or raw garlic in the bag -** These are not really suggested as they do not add much to the cook and in some instances can hurt it. Butter and oils can leech more fat from the meat, making it less flavorful. Fresh herbs and garlic only season where they touch the meat, so it is usually better to use dried versions. Raw garlic has the possibility to grow botulism in the bag during cooking also.

- **Do Not sous vide in store packaging** - This is one of the most frequently asked questions in some of the online sous vide groups. Store packaging may or may not be sanitary, may have unseen holes, may not be temperature rated, and a whole host of other reasons why it does not make sense. It is always best to re-vacuum pack all foods. This also gives you the ability to pre-season.

- **Plan way ahead of time** - Sous vide takes a lot more time than most other cooking methods. It is not something you can usually decide to do last minute unless it is something like seafood or some thin steaks. Make sure you plan ahead as much as possible and not try to rush things.

- **When do I season the meat?** - This will boil down to personal preference. I usually season a little before and a little after the sous vide cook and before searing/smoking. Salt is always a good idea pre-sous vide as it will brine the meat.

This should give you a good base to understand Sous Vide going forward.

Fire & Water Cooking

CHAPTER 3

WHY COMBINE THE METHODS?

So why take these two awesome cooking methods and combine them? There are several very good reasons to do so for sure. I touched on a couple already in the previous chapters, but I will go into a little more detail here. You will see it a little more once you get into the recipes that will more properly demonstrate some of proper techniques. But for now, here are a few reasons for "Sous Vide Que" as Meathead Goldwyn of AmazingRibs.com has dubbed it.

- **Sous Vide is not really a "complete" cooking method on its own for most things -** When cooking proteins like steak, chicken, ribs, brisket and pork roasts, sous vide leaves the exterior rather dull and gray. The meat will be perfectly cooked inside, but you really need to finish the exterior with either a sear or build up a bark. With vegetables, seafood, and some other foods, you can get away with not adding the "finishing" step, but not with most meats.

  You really need a good sear or some smoke time to make that -Maillard reaction- we discussed in earlier chapters. That golden brown, crusty, flavorful finish we all know and love. For smoke flavor, you could put a little "liquid smoke" in the bag if you wish, but I find that overpowering and you still need to sear it anyway, so why not just smoke it outside? You can definitely finish searing or browning on the stove or in an oven, but why do that when you have more and better options?

- **The ability to make moister meats -** Remember one of the major benefits of sous vide is the ability to make moister meats. This holds true for when you are mixing the cooking methods as well. If you have ever done any low and slow barbecue, you are familiar with "The Stall", that point in the cook where the internal temperature stops raising for a good amount of time. That is caused by something known as "evaporative cooling". This is when moisture is leaving the meat cooling the surface and the rest of the interior, very similar to what happens when we sweat.

  Usually this starts happening when the internal temperature of the meat gets to around 150f/65.55c or more. Up until then, the meat is retaining much more moisture than it does later in the cook. Once the meat gets past this point the internal temperature and moisture loss will accelerate drying the meat out. When we mix the methods, we are usually not wanting to exceed the internal temperatures we had cooked to during the sous vide portion and since most sous vide cooks use temperatures lower than 150f/65.55c you will end up with a much moist end product. Another reason would be the lack of evaporation during cooking since it is cooked in a sealed bag.

- **The ability to tenderize at much lower temperatures -** In my humble opinion, this is the BEST reason to combine the two cooking methods for tough meats! It was the original reason that got me all excited when I first started experimenting. Using sous vide and barbecue is the ONLY way you can make a super tender Smokey beef brisket, and have it cooked to medium-rare doneness. Beef ribs are another perfect example of something that can be done this way. Have you ever tried to make Top Round (aka London Broil) on the grill where it was anywhere near tender without having to cut it really thin? Pretty much any tough cut of red meat including beef, veal, lamb, bison, venison, elk, etc. can benefit from these processes while being able to have a great medium-rare to medium doneness. This is something you just cannot do any other way!

- **Convenience -** Yes, I said it. This is a big reason that sous vide barbecue makes a lot of sense for most people. Yes, you are still cooking for a long time, but you do not have to stay on top of the fire. Back before the new fancy WIFI and Bluetooth pit temperature controllers, you pretty much had to babysit you smoker overnight making sure the fire stayed going, the smoker wood stayed smoking, and it didn't get too hot. Even now with all the technology you have to make sure you have enough fuel, and your power does not go out.

  Granted, the sous vide circulators run on electricity also, if you are cooking in an insulated container you have little to worry about losing a large piece of meat due to it being in the danger zone for hours. I feel very comfortable dropping a 20-pound brisket into a water bath for 48 hours plus and sleeping like a baby during the cook. Now I do admit you do have to plan out your cooks a little more since you are going for longer amounts of time, but this is pretty easy if you are already used to doing long cooks on the smoker.

- **Bulk Cooking -** This could also be included in the last section, but sous vide makes it much easier on large cooks if you have the right equipment. You easily cook several large briskets or pork butts in a large cooler with a strong enough circulator (or two). After sous vide cooking you can chill it down and then keep it in the fridge for a few days before you finish it on the smoker. That can save you time on the day you are cooking since it only takes a couple hours to get the meat reheated and the bark developed. It can also save you some clean up time as a lot of the fat is rendered in the sous vide bag.

- **Reheating Leftover Traditional Cooks** - Yes, you can ask any barbecue champion who has ever used sous vide to reheat leftover brisket or pork butt, they will tell you the same thing. Sous vide is perfect for re-heating since it is precise temperature cooking, is done in a water bath, and it is so easy to toss your frozen leftovers directly from the freezer into the bath. And it takes very little time to reheat due the increased heat transfer!

Sous vide can do many more things such as infusions, cryo-concentrations, fermentations, and even help with brewing beer! But in this book, we are going to focus on why it works so well when combined with barbecue and grilling. If you are interested in learning more about what else sous vide can be used for, check out chapter 10 for more resources.

Fire & Water Cooking

CHAPTER 4

GRILLS, SMOKERS, AND OTHER OUTDOOR COOKERS

In the last several years, the outdoor cooking space has exploded with new types of cookers, technology, and accessories. I don't know if it is the demand driving the innovation, or the innovation driving the demand, but either way, the market *and* options have grown at an amazing clip. Most of you reading this more than likely have a grill or smoker of some kind on your patio, but I wanted to touch on what is currently available out there right now and how it can work with sous vide. I am not a big proponent of single use type cookers, so I highly suggest if you are in the market, make sure you consider the overall functionality of a cooker.

One thing I always like to suggest to those who are looking for a new outdoor cooker, do not just look at price. Make sure it will last a long time and do what you want it to do, as there are enough choices out there now you don't have to settle for cheap junk. Do some research before spending the money. Make sure you understand the different fuels such as gas, charcoal, wood, pellets, etc. and how easy it is to use wood for smoke. I am of the opinion that there is a place for all types of cooking fuels, but I prefer to use charcoal and wood chunks as I find it easier to control the temperatures and the amount of smoke in my cooks.

Some of you also may not know the difference between a smoker, a grill, and products that can do it all, so I will address all of this in the breakouts below:

- **Grills** – These can run from a basic propane grill, charcoal kettle, hibachi, fire pit, or those things you see at the local park or campground that are cemented into the ground. These are usually used just for hot and fast grilling, but some can also be used as a smoker if you buy certain accessories. Hot and fast grilling is what they are best at as they can get very hot and produce amazing sears to sous vide steaks and roasts. Most people will have something like this available as they are readily available at the local Walmart or hardware 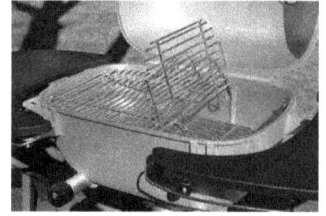 store at affordable prices. You will also find some other grills like "Santa Maria" or "Argentinian" type grills that have adjustable grates that use live fire and coals.

- **Stand Alone Smokers** - You will also find plenty of these types of units at the local store that either use electric, charcoal, propane, or even pellets. These are another type of single type use cooker as they most of the time cannot "grill" but are meant for low and slow smoking only. These look like small refrigerators and use wood chips or pellets to generate the smoke. They are great for chicken, pork, ribs, etc. but not good for steaks, chops, or burgers due to the low temperatures used. I will also include "Bullet" and "Barrel" type smokers in this group as they usually do a horrible job at grilling even though some of them try to sell you on the fact that they can do it. Even if you can, they are usually difficult to set up for it and most don't even try.

- **Offset Smokers** - These are the larger type smokers you see on "BBQ Pitmasters" and other shows. These cookers are very popular in competitions as they are truly "indirect" smokers, since the fire   :ate from the cooking pit. The fire box is "off-set" or i different part of the cooker and the smoke and h flow over and under the meat and out the smokesta You will find some of these smokers that may or n not have some grill grates and ability to use the fire k to grill, but there is usually very limited space on These types of smokers take a lot of practice to le how to use and they require a lot of attention when using them. I would not recommend this type for a beginner for sure.

- **Multi-Purpose Type Cookers -** There are a few types of cookers that will fall into this category for sure. They make it easy to switch from grilling to smoking, direct and indirect heat, and can also bake, cook pizza, use rotisseries, griddling, and more. Here a few styles of cookers that can be considered multi-purpose including some brand names:

- Ceramic Kamado Cooker (Big Green Egg, Kamado Joe, Vision, etc.)
- Metal "Box Type" Cookers (Hasty Bake, M Grills, PK Grill, Weber Kettle, Masterbuilt Gravity series, etc.)
- Some Pellet Cookers (Camp Chef, Weber SmokeFire).

There are many more out there for sure. The main thing you are looking for is just how easy it is for the particular cooker to go from smoking, to grilling, to griddling, to baking with as few extra accessories as possible. **Having a versatile cooker on your patio will make sure you have much more fun cooking outside!**

- **Flat Top Griddles, etc.** - The last couple years there has been a huge growth of these types of cookers and more manufacturers are releasing their own models. These are very versatile and can be used with so many different foods and styles. They are great for such things as searing steaks, stir fry's, smash burgers, breakfast, sandwiches, and much more. Some of these cookers even have deep fryers and warming drawers built into them.

- **Accessories, Gear, and other Gadgets -** Besides all the awesome cookers you have available to you now, the number of accessories and gadgets also continues to grow. I could probably write a whole other book just on this subject alone! The next time you are in your local Mega Hardware store, check out the outdoor cooking area and see for yourself. Wi-Fi/Bluetooth thermometers, pit temperature controllers, Pizza oven attachments, fire starters, torches, racks, you name it. One of the newest products to come out in the last couple years are the totally wireless thermometers such as The MeatStick. It operates with Wi-Fi or Bluetooth and can be used to measure the internal temperature of your food in the sous vide bath as well as on the smoker! You can see many of these products in my Amazon Store here: https://www.amazon.com/shop/fireandwatercooking

For those of you who are looking for more information on all the different types of cookers and accessories out there including reviews, recipes, and much more, visit one of the best outdoor cooking websites on the planet, www.AmazingRibs.com.

What About Fuel Sources?

Propane, natural gas, lump charcoal, charcoal briquettes, real wood logs, wood chips, wood chunks, electric elements, etc. There are many different opinions and options for what you can use in outdoor cookers. I am under the opinion there is a time and place for most all of them. You can't get a good smoke profile without real wood, so you really need that as part of any good "smoking" set up. Below is a good explanation of each with their strengths and weaknesses to consider.

- **Charcoal Briquettes** – probably the most popular fuel source. Made with processed burnt wood and carbon and sometimes with a binder added. Uniform in size, uniform in heat production, usually cheap and readily available. Produces a lot of ash. Some new products now even contain some smoking wood within the charcoal to add more smoke flavor.

- **Lump Charcoal** - Brunt and carbonized pieces of wood left in its natural state and usually has different sizes. Produces less ash than briquettes but can be harder to control the heat due to the different sizes and possibility of some pieces not being fully carbonized.

- **Propane/Gas** - probably the most popular due to the ease of use. Adds no flavor or taste to the food. Easy to adjust the temperatures. Can use accessories to add smoke with wood chips or chunks.

- **Wood Logs/Chips/Chunks** - Using logs alone in a smoker for the fuel source can be hard to control the temperatures and will require lots of attention. Wood chips and chunks can be used with other sources to add smoke.

Lighting Options

Unless you are using an electric or a gas grill/smoker, you will be needing a way to light the fire. I recommend to NEVER use lighter fluid or Match Light type charcoal. Those types of accelerants can add bad tastes, flavors, and unnecessary chemicals to your cook. I recommend using starters made of sawdust and wax, torches, or even charcoal chimney starters. There are also some electric starters that work well. I also prefer the newer super powerful torches such as The GrillGun that allow you to light the grill in a matter of minutes and you can find it here www.grillblazer.com.

Close Proximity Smoking with GrillGrates

My friend Meathead Goldwyn at www.AmazingRibs.com came up with this awesome way to add a little smoke flavor to sous vide food when searing using the GrillGrate brand of grates. These hard cast aluminum grates offer deep channels that have holes in them that allow you to place smoking pellets in the channels and they heat up enough to smoke and add flavor to what you are grilling. You can use any flavor of pellet you choose, but I suggest either a competition blend, oak, or hickory. It works great on steaks, chicken, pork chops, and even vegetables. They have sizes to accommodate just about any grill, so check out the GrillGrates in my Amazon Store here www.amazon.com/shop/fireandwatercooking

What if you don't have a grill or smoker?

Over the years I have had many people asking me how to incorporate smoke into their sous vide cooks if they do not have a smoker. You could use liquid smoke in the sous vide bag when cooking, but you really have to be careful as it is very easy to overpower your food. Other options are using a smoking gun, smoked salt and other smoked seasonings such as what FreshJax offers. You could also make a makeshift smoker in your oven by using disposable aluminum pans and wood chips. Doing a quick google search will find a few different methods on how to do this.

Fire & Water Cooking

CHAPTER 5
SOUS VIDE EQUIPMENT AND ACCESSORIES

Just like in the outdoor cooking sector, the indoor cooking technology has also grown and changed in the last few years. As I addressed, earlier sous vide circulators used to be thousands of dollars and were not affordable for the average home cook. As the word got out just what sous vide could do for cooking, companies started popping up to make affordable solutions for the regular cook. I remember hearing the stories of people making DIY sous vide cookers out of old crock pots and devices that shut the power on and off to control the temperature of the water.

We are lucky now to have so many options of lower cost products with things like Wi-Fi and Bluetooth controls and applications that have many recipes and other helpers for people who are new to the method. There are even products now that offer the ability to keep your food cold during the day and start the cook when you choose without even being home! As with all equipment, you need to do a little research on the brands and options they provide as well as the quality and customer service they provide instead of just cost. I am also going to include some information on vacuum sealers in this chapter as many people will use them with sous vide cooking. So, let's dive into some of the stuff available.

- **All in One Sous Vide Bath -** some of the first sous vide units that became available were sous vide "Bath" units made by companies such as "Sous Vide Supreme" that were not circulators, but a static sized bath that heats the water from the bottom and side like a traditional crock pot. The main drawback to these types of units is the limited capacity of them. You have to be able to fit the amount and type of food you are cooking within the interior of the unit. 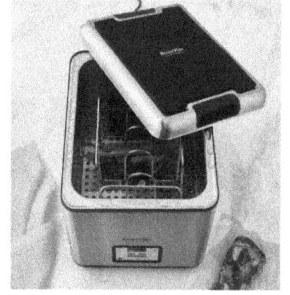 Another issue is the possibility of the water temperature not being as even as the water that is constantly being circulated through the heat source of a Circulator.

- **Sous Vide Stick Circulators -** These are the most popular and more versatile sous vide cooking devices. They can fit most any size container, a lot of them offer powerful heaters and circulators that can handle large amounts of water. Many offer the ability to control them manually or with wireless apps and have built in recipes and other guides to help you use them successfully. I highly recommend if you are looking to use sous

vide with barbecue you look at some of the circulators that offer at least 1,000 watts of power as you will be cooking larger cuts for longer cook times. Also, make sure you choose a well-known company with a great reputation for customer service. Some of the brands I recommend are Anova Culinary, Inkbird, Vesta Precision, and Joule. The only issue I have with the Joule circulator is there are no manual controls. You must use your phone or other mobile device to operate it.

- **Hybrid Type Circulators Bath Combination with Cooling -** Although these types of units seem to be trying to solve a problem that the busy, active home cook has with sous vide cooking, they seem to have some issues. The Mellow Sous Vide was marketed as having the ability to keep your food cold in the bath until you had it start cooking while you were at work. From the beginning the technology that they used for the cooling function was questionable at best, and there were many who doubted that it was actually safe using the units. Another issue they have is the same as the other built-in type units, limited cooking space. I have not  personally used one of these units, so I don't want to throw too many stones, but I do know they recently had an ownership change and they started charging a monthly service fee to use the app that controls the unit, which pretty much makes it impossible to use it unless you pay the monthly fee. People that bought the original units are not happy. There may be some other units like this in the future, but I do not see a big demand for them really.

- **Combi Steam Ovens -** These have been around for a few years but just like sous vide circulators, they started in the commercial kitchens. They have been very expensive and large so not very practical to have in the home, but that is changing with the release of the new [Anova Precision Oven](). These ovens use steam to replicate the sous vide bath and can do a very good job with other functions like convection cooking as well. Many high-end restaurants use these in place of sous vide baths as  they are easier to work with to some extent. You do have some issues with size limitations and usability for certain purposes though, like infusions and other things. As of this writing the Anova Precision Oven is just starting to be shipped so there are not many reviews and long-term tests to see how it will hold up, but it looks very promising as another avenue for sous vide cooking at home. You can check out my podcast episode with Scott Heimendinger, Chief Marketing Officer of Anova on my YouTube channel here to learn more https://youtu.be/5lmc8jFkt9A

- **Sous Vide Containers and Racks -** Containers are a necessity for sure, but the good thing is you have a lot of choices for them. There are purpose-built containers from a few different companies such as Anova Culinary, Lipavi, and Everie of different sizes that have lids that are custom fit for certain circulators, but you have other options. When I first started out to test sous vide I just used a stock pot I already had. Now I have several different sized containers for different types of cooks. As long as you use something sturdy, that won't leak, and you can cover to avoid evaporation, you can use just about anything. I do love my Anova Pro Stainless container because it is insulated, and looks awesome, but I also use a cheap Coleman Stacker cooler with a hole drilled in the lid that works amazing for large racks of ribs, full packer briskets, and large pork butts.

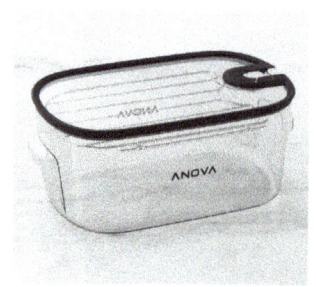

Whichever container you choose, make sure you are not over filling it with food so that the water can do its job. You need to have enough free space for the water to flow around the meat to evenly cook it. There are also racks available to keep food separated and also from floating to the top of the water. You will have to decide for yourself if you need these as I have not found I use mine much. One word of caution I would like to give you though, whatever container you use, make sure you do not put it directly on your granite or other stone type countertop without some kind of trivet or pad underneath it. I have seen expensive granite countertops develop cracks after being directly exposed to the heat over long periods of time. Besides containers, you can also find custom fitting lids for stockpots, plastic sous vide balls that can be used in various different containers to prevent or slow evaporation, and many different weights to hold bags under the water during cooking.

- **Internal Thermometers -** There are now companies like Thermoworks, Polyscience, Vacmaster, and several others that are either making needle-type internal thermometers that can penetrate the sous vide bag without allowing water in so you can monitor the temperature of the meat during the cook. Some of these are incorporated into more expensive commercial type circulators and meant to 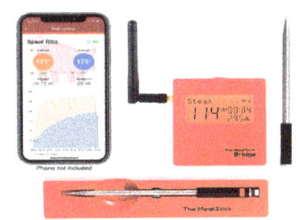 be used in the food service industry to comply with local health department plans. There are also some 100% wireless thermometers now like The MeatStick that are waterproof that can also monitor the internal temperature of your meat in the bag via WIFI. These are not necessary to cook sous vide, but they come in handy when cooking large items for shorter times so you can see if the food has been pasteurized by calculating how long the food has been at the final cooking temperature.

- **Vacuum Sealers and other bags -** Nowadays there are many options for vacuum sealing food. You can start at small hand pumps that use special zipper bags with a sealable hole, to commercial type chamber sealers and all points in between. I do not recommend the hand pump type bags as I have found they tend to leak a lot in sous vide cooking. Also, I do not recommend the reusable silicone bags you will find out there as they are hard to clean and will also leak. I do highly recommend getting a decent vacuum sealer if you plan on using sous vide on a regular basis. One thing to understand with vacuum sealers when it comes to barbecue type meats is the size. You would be hard pressed to get a large bone-in pork shoulder or packer brisket to fit into a chamber sealer bag, primarily because they are limited in size, so they'll fit inside the unit itself.

Channel type sealers, on the other hand, suction the air in the bag from the outside and have various sizes available. You can even find expandable bag rolls that are pleated and allow you to customize them for much larger items than normal zipper or vacuum bags. You can use zipper type bags if you wish, but I find I use vacuum sealers much more for food storage, so it pays for me to use a real vacuum sealer. Chamber sealers for the home user are also getting much more affordable these days. Chamber vacuum sealers remove the air from the entire "chamber" that the bag sits in, so you get a much better vacuum than a channel sealer and you do not need the more expensive textured bags that channel type suction sealers require so that it can remove as much air as possible.

- **Circulator stands, cases, and more -** As with most things, there are many other accessories made that do not add to the cooking ability of sous vide. Stands to hold circulators, portable carrying cases, bag clips for zipper bags, insulation sleeves for containers, and much more. Check out my Amazon Store to see the many things you can buy to customize your sous vide experience, LOL!

If you are in need of sous vide equipment, make sure to check out my Amazon Store where you will find some of my favorite picks. I also have a few reviews and comparison videos on there, as well.

https://www.amazon.com/shop/fireandwatercooking

Now that we discussed a lot of equipment, let's get into some cooking details.

CHAPTER 6

HOT & FAST SOUS VIDE BARBECUE COOKING TIPS

I thought I would separate the processes I use with sous vide when incorporating it into hot and fast grilling and low and slow cooking so I can explain the differences in more detail so you can better understand the reasons for each. Some of the questions that I get most often in the online groups relate to the differences in each of these types of cooks. Just like the different techniques you have in the traditional cooking methods, the same holds true when using sous vide. I consider any sous vide cook that is <u>under six hours</u> a hot and fast cook.

Reason being you are usually not trying to tenderize the meat much, you are just trying to pasteurize and get it cooked all the way through. Also, you are generally not adding a lot of smoke like you would in a brisket or pork butt cook, you are looking more for a good sear and Maillard reaction crust, or a nice crispy skin on poultry. There are some different ways to incorporate "Fire" in a hot and fast cook, so let's take a look at them.

Direct Heat - Just like the name suggests, this method puts your food directly over or on the heat source. This can be from either Convective or Radiant heat, but not Convection. This can be done in a few different ways of course, so I will list of few so you can get an idea of what we are talking about:

- Open flame or charcoal on a grill (also see Close Proximity Smoking on page 25)
- Open flame on a Charcoal Chimney with a grill grate
- High powered torch
- Hot pan on a grill or burner
- Griddle or flat top grill

Using direct heat can be tricky as you are combining higher heat with direct flame a lot of times. Be careful not to burn your meat or overcook it by searing it too long. Personally I do not like the "Grill Marks" look on steaks or chops either. Although the crosshatch marks can look cool, getting an overall crust on your meat will add much more flavor!

Indirect Heat - So, opposite of direct heat, this type uses Convection heat from the air, more like a smoker or pellet grill. The air is heated and moves around the food cooking it evenly. Pellet grills and convection ovens push the heated air around with a fan, but some other grills like Ceramic Kamados (Big Green Egg, etc.) and others rely on the shape of the grill to accomplish the same thing. Anyway, the heat source is blocked or covered. This is the same process used in low and slow cooking, but the temperatures are hotter.

So, what do I use each one of these different methods on my sous vide food? Well, that is not an easy question to answer because you can use either of these for a lot of different foods and it all just depends on what finish you are going for on each individual cook. The recipes I have included in this book will give examples of this, but here is a basic list to get you started.

Direct Heat	Indirect Heat
Steaks	Whole Chicken
Burgers	Most Skin on Poultry
Chicken	Roasts
Pork Chops	Pork Chops
Fish and Seafood	Ribs
Sausages	Steaks when using "Reverse Sear"
Roasts	Side Dishes
Vegetables	

For these hot and fast type cooks I have a certain process that I find works best for my sous vide cooks. Feel free to experiment and customize to suit your own personal tastes and cooking styles for sure but give these a try and see if you like it!

Types of meat that work well with Hot & Fast

All your more tender cuts are best as they do not need the longer times necessary to tenderize them.

- **Beef** – Rib eye, filet, T-bone, strip steak, Denver steak, flat iron, top sirloin, hanger steak, tri tip, top sirloin cap, petite tender, prime rib, strip roast, flank
- **Lamb** – Loin chops, leg of lamb, T-bones,
- **Pork** – tenderloin, loin,
- **Poultry** – all except duck and goose
- **Seafood** – all

Hot and Fast Sous Vide Techniques

- For thinner steaks and chops - ice bath them for a couple minutes before searing to avoid overcooking.
- Dry the Food - make sure you dry the food off as much as possible before searing.
- Be careful not to over sear your meat - flip after 30-40 seconds. You can go a little longer on thicker cuts.
- Seasoning - season a little before and a little after the sous vide bath. Be careful not to over-season.
- Use powdered herbs and garlic instead of fresh - you'll get better overall seasoning of the meat that way. Fresh herbs will only season where they touch the meat.
- Pre-searing - can be used for meats that you may not have a chance to sear after the sous vide bath.
- Avoid adding butter or other oils in the bag - it does not add anything to the flavor of the food. Use it for searing for a much better result.
- Avoid using marinades - especially marinades with vinegar or ingredients like citrus or pineapple that can over-tenderize your meat.
- Use a little oil in searing to get a better crust - higher smoke point oils work best. Try a thin coating of mayonnaise some time for an amazing result.
- Use some wood chips or pellets - toss them in the fire right before searing to get a little smoke on your meat.
- Get it Hot - make sure you wait until your surface or fire is over 500f/260c before searing
- Wait to Glaze - if you are going to use a finishing glaze or sauce, wait until you get a good crust first.
- Want to add some smoke? Check out "Close Proximity Smoking" on page 25.
- High heat for crispy skin - when trying to get crispy skin, make sure your temperature is about 375f/190c or higher before putting the meat on.
- Spray it down - use a little spray oil on roasts or poultry to help crisp the skin.
- Avoid Sticking - pre-oil your grill grates to avoid sticking.
- Save the bag juices - you can make amazing sauces and gravies from these.

Feel free to print this page or make a copy to keep handy as a reference sheet.

CHAPTER 7
LOW & SLOW SOUS VIDE BARBECUE COOKING TIPS

This is where I think combining sous vide and barbecue really shines in my opinion and is what got me excited when I got my first circulator. Sous vide is really the "Ultimate Low & Slow" as it goes generally lower and much longer than traditional barbecue times and temperatures. But it does lack the ability to create an awesome smoky bark on its own, so it does need a little help. As I have said before, when mixing these processes together, you can get an end result that you cannot get ANY other way or with each method on their own!

Unlike hot & fast cooking, low & slow is mostly done with "indirect" heat. You will find some traditional barbecue restaurants where they cook things in huge cement block pits over hot coals where the meat is a good three feet or more away from the heat, but us home cooks mostly use indirect cooking. Even with those types of pits, they are mostly using "convection" heat to cook with at lower temperatures, so indirect heat is what I will focus on.

With that in mind, there are still some best practices I have found over the years that work better than others. Although, like any type of cooking you will get people who do things a little different and find ways that they like better personally for whatever reason. I am not going to debate personal preference here, but I am going to point out some fact-based reasons why I feel certain techniques work better than others.

Incorporating sous vide with your traditional smoking meats like brisket, beef ribs, and chuck roasts offers you a much wider doneness range than you have cooking on the smoker alone. Tough meats can now be cooked medium rare while still being super tender and smoky. You will find several recipes in this book that highlight this amazing ability.

Just like with traditional barbecue and low and slow cooking, there are plenty of myths, legends, opinions, and just plain misinformation out there on just what is the best way to incorporate smoke with sous vide cooking and I must say I have tried them all. I am not one who likes to add extra or unnecessary steps to a cook if they do not add any particular benefit to the end result. But I do like to experiment and test out new ideas that make sense and are based on facts.

Types of meat that work well with Low & Slow - All your more tough cuts are best as they need the longer times necessary to tenderize them. These are harder working muscles that get more blood flow also, so they can be more flavorful and beefier than more tender cuts. These will also contain more connective tissue and collagen that can be broken down and turned into gelatin over the longer cooking times. That is one of the reasons these cuts can be juicier the longer they are cooked even though more water is being expressed. This is why you can sometimes have a dry brisket flat if not cooked long enough or hot enough. It is not overcooked, but actually undercooked.

- **Beef** – brisket, short ribs, top round, bottom round, sirloin tip, navel, shank, chuck steaks and roasts, chuck eye, skirt, cheeks, plate ribs, back ribs
- **Lamb** – ribs, shoulder, shank
- **Pork** – shoulder, Boston butt, picnic, spareribs, baby back ribs, shank
- **Poultry** – duck and goose can go longer times
- **Game Meat** - most game meat cuts except the backstrap or tenderloin.

Check out the list of techniques on the next page and keep them handy. These are some of the things I have experimented with the most and found what works best for me and my family. A lot of it is based on science and fact, but some is personal preference. Try it my way first, then feel free to experiment on your own.

Low & Slow Sous Vide Techniques

- **Smoke after sous vide -** This is a popular topic debated heavily in the sous vide groups. My technique is as follows - sous vide, chill, and put on smoker cold and wet as it makes superior bark. Pre-smoking will work, but you will damage the bark and wash off some smoke flavor in the bag juices. Smoke will NOT penetrate deep into the meat. Meathead Goldwyn from www.AmazingRibs.com agrees with me. With pre-smoking you will just damage the bark and remove smoke during the sous vide cook.
- **Trim more fat than you would for a traditional cook -** you will not need a fat cap to help protect the meat from long term exposure to high heat, so trim as much as possible so you can get more bark and seasoning on the surface.
- **Chill the meat before smoking -** This will accomplish two things, it will give you more time to help develop the bark and smoke without going over the original cooking temperature, and cold wet meat attracts much more smoke.
- **Do not dry the meat off -** This is the exact opposite of the advice I give for hot and fast cooking. When smoking, cold wet meat helps develop the bark and attracts more smoke. Add a little more seasoning and keep it wet!
- **Spritz the meat a couple times during smoking -** Smoke cannot stick much to dry surfaces. To help develop bark and attract more smoke, spritz with any type of liquid every 20 minutes or so. The type of liquid does not matter much.
- **Do Not Overcook -** Throw out the old doneness temperatures you used to use with just cooking on the smoker.
- **Use a meat thermometer to monitor internal temperature -** This will allow you to make sure you do not overcook and dry out the meat.
- **Save and repurpose the bag juices -** This is another great thing about cooking sous vide. You can use the bag juices, also known as the "Purge", to make gravies, stocks, and sauces. You can also add them back to the meat with something like pulled pork or beef!
- **Experiment with times and temperatures -** The many doneness ranges with times and temperatures will expand your options, so I suggest you try a few different ones to see what you like!

Feel free to print this page or make a copy to keep handy as a reference sheet.

Fire & Water Cooking

CHAPTER 8
CONVERTING TRADITIONAL RECIPES AND OTHER DETAILS

Believe it or not, it is not hard at all to convert traditional recipes to incorporate sous vide. The main thing you really have to take into consideration is the extra time it takes compared to other methods. I can't tell you how many times I have heard statements like "are you crazy cooking something for 48 hours?" or something similar.

The second thing you need to understand is the lower cooking temperatures that can be used compared to traditional methods. The rest of the steps are just nuances that can change or be adjusted and experimented with to tweak to your personal preference. Here is a brief list to keep in mind when converting recipes.

- **Determine the time and temperature -** Make sure to consult a trusted source for times and temperatures. I highly suggest you check a couple different sources as you will find different results as there are many opinions on these. One of the sources I trust the most is my friend Jason Logsdon's guide on Amazingfoodmadeeasy.com as he uses "ranges" on all foods and gives information on how to calculate them based on thickness.

- **Determine the finishing method you will use -** This should be one of the easier things to figure out as they usually don't change. Steaks and chops will be seared, brisket and pork butt low and slow, etc. Just keep in mind the other things we discussed in earlier chapters for the method you are using.

- **Search for current sous vide recipes for what you are doing -** Since sous vide has been getting more and more popular, there is most likely a recipe out there for what you are looking to cook or convert already. Do a Google search or check out the many websites like Serious Eats or ChefSteps.

- **Season a little before and a little after -** This will make sure you get a much better overall flavor profile.

You can also cook some of the recipes in this book to get your head wrapped around the methods and techniques that work best with sous vide and barbecue and then you can start to experiment on your own. Just make sure you are taking into consideration the issues that can come up due to the nature of sous vide cooking in general:

- **Use safe cooking practices -** Do not leave food in the bath at temperatures lower than 126f/52.22c for long periods of time. Make sure you follow credible sources with proven pasteurization tables instead of using your own judgment. I highly recommend Douglas Baldwin's book ["Sous Vide for the Home Cook"](#).

- **Make sure you use the correct bags** - Use food safe bags such as Zipper type "Freezer" bags or vacuum sealer bags. Also make sure you have the proper size for what you are cooking.
- **Don't overfill your sous vide container** - Remember that you want the water to be able to circulate around the food as much as possible, so don't over fill the container to inhibit the flow of water. You also do not want the food floating to the top outside of the water.
- **Make sure you use a lid or cover** - if too much water evaporates from your container, it can damage your circulator and also affect the results of your cook.
- **Understand that you can overcook using sous vide** - You CAN overcook food using sous vide. Although it is a little different from traditional cooking, since the process tenderizes proteins over time, you can turn meat into mush even at lower temperatures by going too long. Be cautious with already tender cuts like tenderloin and other types of meat.
- **Do not go over the sous vide cooked temperature when smoking** - This is one of the hardest things that "Barbecue Guys" can't get their heads around, you no longer need to cook the brisket and pork butt over 200f to get tender. Sous vide uses the longer time and lower temperature to tenderize so the traditional times you would use in regular low and slow barbecue do not apply.
- **There is no need to "Rest" your meat** - With sous vide cooking you are using a static temperature over a long period of time. This means there is no "carry-over" cooking to worry about or juices that need to redistribute due to the higher cooking temperatures of traditional cooking. The searing process, if done correctly, should not raise the internal temperature of the meat at all.
- **Understand that different foods cook differently** - Meats and other proteins cook much differently than vegetables. You can cook a steak at 130f/54.44c for 3 hours and have it turn out perfect but try cooking carrots at 134f/54.4c and they will not cook at all no matter how long they sit in the bath. Different cell structures require different times and temperatures, so follow credible well-known recipes.
- **Doneness level ranges** - Although doneness is a big personal preference issue, there are some details you should consider when looking at different types of meat or cuts when looking at doneness temperatures, especially on red meat. For example, medium-rare on a lean filet mignon may be perfect at 128-131f, but for steaks like ribeye may be better at 134-135f due to the fat and connective tissue being able to render better at the slightly hotter temperature. Beef fat for instance does not start to render until it hits these temperatures. This is one reason why I

like recipes and time/temperature charts that use ranges instead of single numbers. Make sure to see the "references and resources" section later in this book for more information.

Once you get used to the little differences and basic principles of sous vide cooking, you will feel more comfortable experimenting on your own and creating amazing food. The recipes in the next section will help you understand the processes that work well with sous vide and barbecue, but don't be afraid to play around with them to make them your own. The time and temperatures for sous vide cooking have a wide range that makes it much more versatile than any other cooking method so you can explore and find the ones that are right for your culinary palate.

Now it's time to get into some basic and some not so basic recipes to help you put those principles and techniques into practice!

CHAPTER 9

BASIC RECIPES AND TECHNIQUES

As I said at the beginning of this book, it is not really a recipe book, but a book of cooking methods and techniques with some recipes in it to help demonstrate those concepts. I have compiled a few recipes here that I have done over the years and some of them can be found on my YouTube channel in video form. I have tweaked and experimented with these to get them just right for my personal tastes.

You will not find much that is super groundbreaking in them, but you may find some ideas to get you interested to try something new by incorporating sous vide and barbecue. No fancy plating, no side dishes or desserts, just some great basic sous vide and barbecue recipes to get you started on the process. The great thing with these recipes is they are all very simple and can be adjusted for your personal taste.

I have been using FreshJax Organic seasonings and blends for over 2 years now and they are fantastic! They offer many different spice blends, rubs, and seasoning mixes along with individual spices. All are the highest quality, fully organic, no artificial flavors, colors, preservatives, anti-caking agents, or GMO's. They are a family run company out of Jacksonville, Florida and truly care about their community. They work closely with charities and donate money from every sale to help end childhood hunger by donating over 176,201 meals since 2011! I use FreshJax organic seasonings exclusively in the recipes in this book and my own personal kitchen.

Like most real people, I do not have the time, money, or energy to load up on fresh herbs from the grocery store every other day or tend to my own herb garden. FreshJax offers high quality products that make me feel good about using dried ingredients! Check out the FreshJax Organic Seasonings here http://freshjax.refr.cc/darrin

Appetizers & Finger Foods

Great for parties, gameday, and other get-togethers

Bacon Wrapped Moink Balls

These usually go really fast when I make these for church socials and family get togethers. Bacon, Meatballs, smoke and sauce, what more can you ask for? The main thing that sous vide can bring to these lovely little morsels is even cooking and much more juicy meatballs. Cooking the meatballs and bacon together in the bath makes sure there is much more even cooking on the smoker after. Once you make these you will never go back to the old way of dried out meatballs!

Prep time: 40 minutes **Cook Time:** 3 1/2 hours **Serves:** 10-15

Ingredients
2 lb ground beef 80/20
2 tbs FreshJax Grill Master rub
3 tbs FreshJax Rosy Cheeks Rub
2 tbs FreshJax Smoky Southwest Rub
2 tbs FreshJax Toasted Onion
1 lb sliced bacon
2 tbs Worcestershire sauce
2 eggs
½ cup of breadcrumbs
2 cups barbecue sauce

Directions
Pre-heat the sous vide bath to 148f/64.44c

Add the ground beef, eggs, breadcrumbs, and Worcestershire sauce into a large bowl.
Mix 1 tbs of the grill master, rosy cheeks, smoky southwest, and toasted onion into the bowl with the meat and mix thoroughly.

Roll into golf ball sized portions.

Cut the bacon slices in half and wrap the meatballs with the half slices. Toothpick if needed.

Place the wrapped meatballs in the freezer and let freeze for one hour.

Vacuum seal the meatballs and place in the sous vide bath for 2 hours.

Remove from the bath and season with the remaining seasoning.

Place in the smoker at 325f/162.77c until crisp, about 40 minutes. Glaze with the sauce and place back on the smoker for another 10 minutes.

Serve and enjoy!

Smoked Deep-Fried Baby Backs

Yep, you saw the title right! I got inspired to do this recipe awhile back when I saw one of the top barbecue competitors I follow do a similar recipe. He just fried them, but I figured I could add some smoke and use sous vide to tenderize them a little more! These are a great appetizer or snack, but you could make a meal out of them also. They literally melted in my mouth when I ate these. I pre-smoked these before the sous vide bath, something that I don't normally do, but since I was not looking to get a bark on them and was finishing by deep frying, it made it easier in the end. You can use pretty much any dipping sauce you like.

Prep time: 30 minutes **Cook Time:** 26 hours **Serves:** 6-8

Ingredients
2 racks of baby back pork ribs
2 tbs FreshJax Rosemary Lemon Sea Salt
2 tbs FreshJax Smokey Southwest Seasoning
2 tbs FreshJax Rosy Cheeks Rub
3 cups all-purpose flour
3 tbs corn starch
2 eggs & 3 tbs water
2 quarts vegetable oil for frying

Directions
Pre heat your smoker to about 225f/107c and use some pecan or hickory wood.

Remove the membrane from the back of the ribs. Season them up with half of the seasoning and place on the smoker for 30 minutes.

Pre-heat your sous vide bath to 155f/68.3c

Remove from the smoker and let rest for 10-15 minutes to cool down.

Vacuum seal the ribs and place in the sous vide bath for 24 hours.

Pre-heat the frying oil to 375f/190c

Mix the flour, corn starch, and remaining seasoning into a large bowl.

Make an egg wash with the eggs and water.

Remove the ribs from the bags. Cut into individual pieces. Dip the ribs in the flour, then the egg, and then the flour again. shake off access flour and toss in the oil.

Let them cook until crispy! Serve and enjoy!

Smoked Pig Wings

What in the world are "Pig Wings" you ask? Well, they are not from flying pigs I can tell you that, LOL! These have been popular on the barbecue competition circuit for a few years now, and I have even had some at Disney's Epcot Center during their annual "International Food and Wine Festival" a couple years ago. These are really pork shanks cut from the smaller lower leg section of the pig. The name came from what they end up looking like when they are cooked, as people say they end up looking like a chicken wing drumette. They may be hard to find, but you can always ask a local butcher. I found mine at www.porterroad.com. This recipe is one of those that you can take in many different directions with different sauces to finish them, so don't be afraid to change the sauces to your own personal taste! It is also very simple and easy to try for something a little different for a meal or appetizer!

Prep time: 30 minutes **Cook Time:** 26 hours **Serves:** 4

Ingredients
6 small pork shanks uncooked

Rub
1 tbs FreshJax Mesquite Lime Sea Salt
2 tbs FreshJax Rosy Cheeks BBQ Rub
1 tbs FreshJax Citrus Pepper seasoning

Directions
Pre-heat the sous vide bath to 150f/65.55c

Season the pork shanks with half of the rub.

Vacuum seal them in the bag. Place the bag into a sous vide bath for 24 hours.

Pre-heat your smoker to 350f/176.66c and add your choice of smoking wood. Place the bags of pork into an ice bath and let cool for 30 to 40 minutes.

Remove pork from bag and place on a wire rack on a sheet pan. Do not dry them off, leave them as wet as possible, Season the pork on both sides with the remaining rub.

Place on the smoker and cook until they have a nice bark or until they reach an internal temperature of 150f/65.55c again.

Serve with your favorite sauce and enjoy!

Smoked Brisket Burnt Ends

Making brisket burnt ends usually is a lot of work cooked traditionally. This recipe shows how you can get a great result with a little less work. With this recipe I start with a full packer brisket that I separate the flat and the point before cooking. You can also cook the entire full packer brisket in the sous vide and separate after the bath and cook them separate. Either way will work, you just need to decide ahead of time what you want to do. I used these burnt ends as a meal in themselves, but you could also use them as an appetizer if you wish. The process is similar to a conventional cook, but you are just adding some time and a little less stress. I have fed these to seasoned barbecue chefs and they would have raved about how juicy they were.

Prep time: 40 minutes **Cook Time:** 38 hours **Serves:** 8-10

Ingredients
One beef brisket point section- fully trimmed
2 tbs FreshJax Smoked Cherry Wood Sea Salt
2 tbs FreshJax Course Black Pepper
1 tbs FreshJax Garlic Herb Blend
3 tbs FreshJax Rosy Cheeks Rub
2 cups barbecue sauce of your choice

Directions
Make sure to trim the brisket point of as much exterior fat as possible. Season the meat with ¼ of the seasoning. Place in the vacuum bag and seal.

Place the meat in a pre-heated sous vide bath of 150f/65.55c and let cook for at least 36 hours.

Before removing the brisket from the bath, get your smoker pre-heated to 275f/135c and add the smoking wood of your choice. I use either oak, pecan, or hickory for beef.

Place the brisket in an ice bath and let chill for at least 40 minutes. Remove from the bag and cut into 1" to 1 ½" cubes. Toss with remaining rub and place on a wire rack on top of a sheet pan. Place in the smoker for 45 minutes until the bark starts to set.

Remove from the smoker and toss them in your favorite barbecue sauce. place back on the smoker for another 15 minutes to set the sauce until it is a thick glaze.

Remove from the smoker, serve and enjoy!

Smoked Hot Chicken Wings

I remember when chicken wings were not a thing. They were born about 1 year before I was in a little bar in Buffalo, NY, about 80 miles from where I was. Now you find them everywhere with thousands of different recipes. Chicken wings are also perfect for sous vide and smoke. So versatile and delicious! Change up the seasonings but the process will get you some awesome wings every time! These are dry rub wings and are very HOT!

Prep time: 15 minutes **Cook Time:** 5 hours **Serves:** 6

Ingredients

5 lbs chicken wings
1 tbs FreshJax Habanero Lime Sea Salt
1 tbs FreshJax Peppered Habanero spice
3 tbs FreshJax Smokey Southwest spice
1 tbs FreshJax Ghost Pepper Sea Salt
Duck fat spray or other spray oil

Directions

Pre-heat the sous vide bath to 148f/64.44c

Season the chicken with half of the seasonings. Bag it up, vacuum seal, and toss it in the bath for 4 hours

Heat up your grill/smoker to about 375f/190.55c and add some pecan wood.

Remove the wings from the bag and dry them off with paper towels as much as possible. Spray the wings with the duck fat or oil

Add the remaining seasoning and place the wings in the grill/smoker over indirect heat.

Cook the wings until they are nice and crispy

Remove from the grill and serve with blue cheese or ranch dressing for dipping!

Enjoy!

Pork Belly Sliders

These will be the hit of any party I guarantee it! Rich, tender, succulent, sweet pork belly, King's Hawaiian rolls, fried jalapenos, Teriyaki Soy Mayo, pickled red onion, who could ask for anything more? If you see the big thick pork belly slices at Costco, that is what I used for this recipe. Use skinless pork belly also. A MUST Try!

Prep time: 40 minutes **Cook Time:** 26 hours **Serves:** 10-15

Ingredients
3 lbs Thick sliced pork belly (1 ½")
2 packages of King's Hawaiian dinner rolls
French's Fried Jalapenos
1 cup pickled red onion

The Rub
4 tbs FreshJax Rosy Cheeks bbq rub
1 tbs FreshJax all-spice
1 tbs FreshJax cinnamon
1 tbs FreshJax Garlic Herb Blend
2 tsp Pink Curing Salt

The Sauce
1 ½ cups mayonnaise
1 tsp ginger
1 tsp all-spice
1 tsp Garlic powder
2 tbs Teriyaki sauce
2 tbs Soy sauce

Directions
Pre-heat the sous vide bath to 150f/65.55c

If the pork belly is not sliced, slice it into 1 ½" thick slices.

Season the pork belly with half the rub on both sides. Place in the vacuum bag and seal it up.

Place the pork belly in the bath and cook for 24 hours.

Heat the smoker up to 275f/135c and add some cherry wood for smoke.

Remove the pork belly from the bag and leave wet. Season with the remaining rub. Place on the smoker for 45 minutes out until they get a nice dark color.

Remove from the smoker and let rest for 5 minutes. Cut the pork belly so they fit good on the rolls.

To build the slider, add the pork belly, the sauce, some French's fried jalapenos, and some pickled red onions, and Enjoy!

Beef Recipes

Roasts, Steaks, Burgers, and More

Coffee Rubbed New York Strip Steaks

What would a sous vide book be without the obligatory steak recipe? Yes, sous vide makes a wonderful steak for sure, especially when you use it for cuts that are not that tender like a strip steak or top sirloin. Here is one of my favorite recipes that will surely impress any steak lover. I usually like a thicker steak as they work better with searing after, so I do these at 1 ½" or more. I used FreshJax Sunrise Cowgirl Coffee Rub on these steaks, and I sprayed them with a little Duck Fat Spray when searing. For a more tender steak, you can cook up to 10 hours.

Prep time: 10 minutes **Cook Time:** 6 hours 10 minutes **Serves:** 4-6

Ingredients
4 New York Strip Steaks 1 ½" thick
1 tbs FreshJax Camp Fire Sea Salt
3 tbs FreshJax Sunrise Cowgirl Coffee Rub
Duck Fat Spray (or any other spray oil)

Directions
Pre-heat the sous vide bath to 130f/54.44c

Season the steaks with half of the rub and place in the vacuum bag and seal.

Cook in the bath for 6 hours or up to 10.

You can sear these anyway you see fit, but I fire up my charcoal grill for these and use Grill Grates brand and flip them over and use the flat surface to get and overall milliard reaction. You can use any flat surface you like. let the surface get to over 500f/260c before putting the steaks on.

Remove the steaks from the bag and dry them off as much as you can.

Season the steaks with the rest of the rub.

Spray the duck fat on the steaks and a little on the searing surface. Place the steaks on and sear for about 30-40 seconds on each side. Flip them a couple times until you get a decent sear color. Be careful not to over sear!

Remove from the grill and let rest for a couple minutes.

Serve and enjoy!

Black Garlic & Coffee Beef Ribs Cooked Medium Rare

This recipe is one that can truly highlight the benefits of combining the cooking methods of sous vide and barbecue. You can use either English cut short ribs or 3 or 4 bone plate beef ribs for this recipe. If you have never had medium rare beef ribs before, you will be in for a treat! The black garlic coffee rub is something I put together last year that I found worked really well on steak, roasts, and just about any kind of beef. If you have never had black garlic, the flavor can be described as a more mellow and sweeter taste than regular garlic. Trim as much surface fat as possible with these as it will not render much in the bath.

Prep time: 20 minutes **Cook Time:** 50 hours **Serves:** 4

Ingredients

1 3 bone rack of plate beef rib or 6 4" cut beef short ribs.
1 tbs FreshJax Rosemary Lemon sea salt
3 tbs Black Garlic Coffee rub (below)
Finishing sauce of your choice!

Black Garlic Coffee Rub

2 tbs FreshJax Pink Salt
2 tbs FreshJax ground black pepper
2 tbs ground black garlic powder
1 tbs FreshJax Garlic Herb Blend
1 tbs fine ground espresso coffee
1 tbs FreshJax onion powder
1 tbs FreshJax ground thyme
1 tbs FreshJax ground rosemary
1 tsp FreshJax cayenne pepper

Directions

Pre heat sous vide bath to 134f/56.66c

Season the ribs with an all-purpose or Salt, Pepper, Garlic rub then seal in the vacuum bag.

Cook in the sous vide bath for 48-56 hours

Pre-heat your smoker to 275f/135c and use some hickory or oak wood. Place bag with ribs in an ice bath for 35-40 minutes while the smoker heats up.

Remove ribs from the bag, leave them wet, season with the Black Garlic Coffee Rub.

Smoke for 45 minutes to one hour or until the internal temperature reaches 134f/56.66c again.

Remove from the smoker and serve!

Big, Thick, Medium Rare Bacon Cheeseburger

I get this question all the time in the online groups, "why would you sous vide burgers?". Well, the best answer I have for that is this type of burger. Sous vide allows to safely make and eat these thick burgers medium rare as it can pasteurize them while not overcooking. No more worrying about getting sick from undercooked ground beef! It also works well for stuffed "Juicy Lucy" burgers as it can make sure the burger is cooked and the cheese melted. Personally, I love a good smash burger, but from time to time I crave a nice, juicy, thick medium rare burger!

Prep time: 10 minutes **Cook Time:** 2 hours 45 minutes **Serves:** 1

Ingredients
¾ lb thick burger patty
2 tsp FreshJax Grill Master Blend
2 slices swiss cheese
2 slices of bacon
1 brioche bun
Sliced onion, tomatoes, pickles, lettuce

Directions
Pre-heat the sous vide bath to 130f/54.44c

There are a couple ways to sous vide your burgers and it all depends on the method you are bagging or the options on your vacuum sealer. If you try and use the factory settings on your vacuum sealer, you may end up squishing your patties too thin. But if your sealer has a "pulse" feature, or an adjustable vacuum time, you can be fine. You can also freeze the patties prior to sealer if you wish.

Some find just using the water displacement method works for them. Whichever way you do it, just make sure they keep their shape.

Season them up with half the grill master blend and toss them in the bath for 2 ½ hours. Why so long? Because they are thick. You need time to pasteurize.

Pre-heat your grill to 500f/260c

Remove burgers from bag and dry them off completely. Season with rest of the seasoning. Cook your bacon to nice and crispy before searing the burgers because they will not take long!

Toss the burger on the grill and sear on both sides for about 1 minute. Throw on the cheese and let it melt. Do not over cook it!

Assemble the burger, serve and enjoy!

Tri Tip Surf and Turf

I live in Florida and it is really hard to find Tri Tip here locally. If you are not familiar with Tri Tip, it is also known as "Bottom Sirloin" because it rests right in between the Top Sirloin and the Sirloin Tip section between the round and sirloin. It is one of my favorite cuts of beef. Be careful when slicing it because the grain runs in 2 different directions. I used some large prawns for this recipe, and it turned out really great!

Prep time: 15 minutes **Cook Time:** 7 hours 15 minutes **Serves:** 6

Ingredients
1 Whole Beef Tri Tip roast
2 lbs of large shrimp or prawns
2 tbs butter

Beef Rub
2 tbs FreshJax Mesquite Lime Sea Salt
2 tbs FreshJax course ground black pepper
2 tbs FreshJax Garlic Herb blend

Shrimp Seasoning
2 tbs FreshJax Fresh Bay Seafood seasoning

Directions
Pre-heat the sous vide bath to 134f/56.66c

Season the tri tip with half of the beef rub. Place in the vacuum sealer bag and seal.

Place the tri tip in the bath and cook for 7 hours. Just before the tri tip is done, season the shrimp with half of the seafood seasoning and bag it up and vacuum seal.

Remove the tri tip from the bath and chill for 10 minutes as you get your grill to searing temperature of 500f. Place the bag of shrimp in the sous vide bath at 134f/56.66c while the meat is cooling.

Remove the tri tip from the bag and add the rest of the beef rub, then sear on the grill, flipping every 3 minutes. Remove from grill.

Add the butter to a hot pan and then add the shrimp. Quickly sear the shrimp in the butter.

Slice up serve and enjoy!

Sous Vide Chuck Eye Steaks

If you can find these, you will thank me after you cook them! There are only like 4 of these per steer and they come from where the chuck roll meets the rib section. You get the best of both worlds here as far a flavor, but sous vide makes them shine more as it can tenderize them a little more while keeping them perfect medium rare. I use a higher heat in the sous vide on these to render more fat and connective tissue.

Prep time: 10 minutes **Cook Time:** 6 hours 10minutes **Serves:** 2-4

Ingredients

2 Chuck Eye Steaks
2 tbs FreshJax Rosemary Lemon Sea Salt
2 tbs FreshJax Citrus Pepper
1 tbs FreshJax Garlic Herb Blend
Duck Fat Spray or other spray oil

Directions

Pre-heat the sous vide bath to 134f/56.66c

Season the steaks with half of the seasonings. Place in the vacuum sealer bag and seal.

Place the steaks in the bath and cook for 6 hours.

Fire up your grill and get it up to at least 500f/260c and we will grill on the grates.

Remove the steaks from the bag and path them dry as much as possible with paper towels.

Hit the steaks with the duck fat spray or other spray oil on both sides. Add the remaining seasoning

Put them on the grill over direct flame.

Make sure to turn the steaks ¼ turn every 10 seconds until you go 360 degrees, then flip them over and do the same on the other side. This will develop a great curst

Let the steaks rest for five minutes. Serve and Enjoy!

Top Round aka London Broil

This is one of my wife's favorite recipes. She is not a big fan of steaks with a lot of fat. I know, what is wrong with her, right? This is normally a very tough cut that takes some expert slicing, marinating, and grilling to try and make it edible, but sous vide to the rescue! This recipe is tender, moist, and flavorful. You may never cook top round any other way again! Please don't give me the old "London Broil is a preparation, not a cut" comments as most grocery stores label it this way.

Prep time: 15 minutes **Cook Time:** 25 hours **Serves:** 6

Ingredients

1 Whole Top Round London Broil
2 tbs FreshJax Mesquite Lime Sea Salt
2 tbs FreshJax Course ground black pepper
1 tbs FreshJax Garlic herb Blend
2 tbs Ghee or Avocado oil
¼ cup red wine
¼ cup beef broth
1 tbs cornstarch

Directions

Pre-heat the sous vide bath to 128f/53.33c

Season the top round with half of the rub. Place in the vacuum sealer bag and seal.

Place the meat in the bath and cook for 24 hours. The longer you go them more tender it gets.

Pre-heat the grill up to 500f/260c. I use a cast iron pan, griddle, or any flat surface.

Remove the meat from the bag and pat dry. Reserve the bag juices to make a sauce with. Add the remaining seasoning to the meat.

Add the bag juices to a pot and heat just to boiling and remove the film from the top. Reduce heat. add a ¼ red wine, ¼ cup beef stock, some salt and pepper, and cornstarch to a bowl and mix. Stir into the pot until it thickens.

Add the oil to the pan/griddle and allow to heat up. Place the meat on and let it sizzle for about 1 minute on each side.

Remove from the heat, slice up and serve with the sauce!

Pastrami Style Beef Short Ribs

These ribs will knock your socks off! They are totally different than anything you have had before and are sure to get rave reviews. I usually serve these with some kind of mustard sauce. They take a little planning and time, but it is well worth it. If you like Pastrami, you will love these!

Prep time: 45 minutes **Cure Time:** 6 days **Cook Time:** 25 hours **Serves:** 6

Ingredients
4 lbs beef short ribs cut into 3-4-inch pieces

Brine
1 gallon of water
1 cup kosher salt
¼ cup brown sugar
2 tsp Prague power #1 (curing salt)
2 tbs pickling spices

Rub
2 tbs course grounds black pepper
1 tbs whole black pepper corns
2 tbs coriander
1 tbs brown sugar
1 tbs paprika
2 tsp onion powder
1 tsp mustard powder
2 tsp garlic powder

Directions
Mix the brine and heat it up for 5 minutes. Let it cool before adding the ribs.

Let them sit in the brine in the refrigerator for 6 days.

Pre-heat the sous vide to 145f/62.77c

Remove the ribs from the brine and wash them off. Add half the rub to the ribs and bag the ribs in vacuum bag. Place in the bath and cook for 24 hours.

Chill the ribs in ice bath for 10 minutes.

Pre-heat the smoker to 275f/135c with cherry wood.

Remove the rib from the bag, leave them wet and add the remaining rub.

Place on the smoking for 45 minutes to one hour until the bark is set.

Remove from the grill and serve with a nice Dijon mustard sauce!

Sous Vide Brisket Cooked Medium

I have to admit, being able to have beef brisket at many different doneness levels AND it be tender is one of my favorite things that sous vide can do. It is fun to make things different ways to see how much different it can be. This will have a different flavor profile than a traditional Texas style brisket for sure. You can experiment with different times and temperatures also! Be sure to trim most of the fat of the exterior as you will not need it to protect the meat like you would traditionally.

Prep time: 20 minutes **Cook Time:** 38 hours **Serves:** 6-8

Ingredients
1 full packer beef brisket
6 tbs FreshJax Camp Fire Sea Salt
3 tbs FreshJax Smokey Southwest
3 tbs FreshJax Course Ground Pepper

Directions

Pre heat sous vide bath to 138f/58.88c

Trim all of the external fat from the brisket and most of the deckle fat.

Season the brisket with half the seasoning and place in an expandable vacuum bag and seal.

Cook in the sous vide bath for 36-48 hours

Pre-heat your smoker to 275f/135c and use some oak wood.

Place bag in an ice bath for 45 minutes while the smoker heats up. You can also toss In the fridge overnight.

Remove the brisket from the bag, leave it wet, and season with the remaining rub.

Smoke for 45 minutes to one hour or until the internal temperature reaches 138f/58.88c again. Spritz the brisket with apple juice of water every 15 minutes to help develop the bark.

Remove from the smoker and let rest for 10 minutes.

Slice up and enjoy!

Santa Maria Tri Tip Roast

Tri Tip is a kind of a regional thing still and it is hard for me to find them around here in Florida. I love them though, so I break down and order them from www.porterroad.com every once in a while. This recipe is kind of a traditional Southern California recipe with a little heat to it. Be careful to slice this with the grain as the grain runs two different way.

Prep time: 10 minutes **Cook Time:** 7 hours **Serves:** 6

Ingredients

1 3 lb Tri Tip roast
2 tbs FreshJax Mesquite Lime Sea Salt
1 tbs FreshJax Peppered Habanero
2 tbs FreshJax Smokey Southwest
1 tbs FreshJax Garlic Herb Blend
1 tbs FreshJax Onion powder
Duck Fat Spray or other spray oil

Directions

Pre-heat the sous vide bath to 134f/56.66c

Season the tri tip with half of the seasonings. Place in the vacuum sealer bag and seal.

Place the tri tip in the bath and cook for 6 hours.

Fire up your grill and get it up to at least 500f/260c and add some oak wood.

Remove the tri tip from the bag and pat them dry as much as possible with paper towels.

Hit the roast with the duck fat spray or other spray oil on both sides. Add the remaining seasoning

Put them on the grill over direct flame.

Make sure to turn the roast frequently to get a uniform crust.

Let the roast rest for five minutes.

Serve and Enjoy!

Bacon Wrapped Stuffed Meatloaf

Also known as a "Fatty" with several different variations, this is one of my favorite things to sous vide and smoke. Sous vide allows the bacon to pre-cook some before smoking to allow it a shorter time to crisp it up while not overcooking the meat. I use two different seasoning profiles on this to make it a little fuller bodied. More savory on the inside and a little sweeter on the outside.

Prep time: 40 minutes **Cook Time:** 7 hours **Serves:** 6-8

Ingredients

2 pounds 80/20 ground beef
1 pound of bacon
1 cup breadcrumbs
¼ cup diced onions
2 eggs
1 ½ cups shredded cheese
1 tsp FreshJax Garlic Herb seasoning
1 tbs FreshJax Camp Fire Smoked salt
2 tsp FreshJax Smokey Southwest
2 tbs FreshJax Rosy Cheeks Rub (exterior only)

Directions

Pre-heat the sous vide bath to 155f/68.33c

Mix the ground beef with the breadcrumbs, eggs, onions, all of the seasoning Except the Rosy Cheeks Rub as that will season the bacon only.

Spread the meat mixture onto a sheet pan into a flat rectangle about ¼ inch thick.

Spread the cheese on the meat until about 1 inch from the edge.

Roll the meat up into a loaf. Create a bacon weave on parchment paper with the bacon and season the top with half bbq rub. Place the meatloaf on the bacon weave and fold the bacon over the loaf, then turn the loaf over with the open part on the bottom.

Season the bacon with half the leftover rub, vacuum seal and toss in the sous vide bath.

Cook for 6 hours in the bath.

Pre-heat smoker to 285f/140.55c and add some pecan wood.

Remove the loaf from the bag, season with the remaining rub, and place on the smoker for 45 minutes or until the bacon crisps up.

Slice and serve!

Prime Rib Roast

Prime rib is a great family pleaser, especially for the holidays. Mixing sous vide and the smoker can make some of the best you have ever made! The perfect temperature, the perfect juiciness, the perfect smokiness, perfect all-around beef roast. This recipe is set for the higher end medium rare doneness to allow for more fat and connective tissue to render.

Prep time: 10 minutes **Cook Time:** 9 hours **Serves:** 6-10

Ingredients

1 Whole Beef rib roast
2 ½ tbs FreshJax Mesquite Lime Sea Salt
1 tbs FreshJax Course ground black pepper
1 tbs FreshJax Garlic herb Blend
1 tbs FreshJax Toasted Onion blend
1 tbs FreshJax Thyme
1 tbs FreshJax rosemary

Directions

Pre-heat the sous vide bath to 134f/56.66c Trim any excess fat cap from the roast

Season the roast with half of the rub. Place in the vacuum sealer bag and seal.

Place the meat in the bath and cook for 8 hours. After removing from the bath place in ice bath

Pre-heat the smoker up to 275f/135c and use a little pecan or hickory wood.

Remove the meat from the bag and leave wet. Reserve the bag juices to make a sauce with.

Add the remaining seasoning to the meat and place on smoker for 45 minutes to 1 hour.

Add the bag juices to a pot and heat just to boiling and remove the film from the top. Reduce heat. add a ¼ red wine, ¼ cup beef stock, some salt and pepper to taste, and 1 tbs of cornstarch to a bowl and mix. Stir into the pot until it thickens.

Remove the roast from the smoker and let rest for 5-10 minutes. Slice and serve with the sauce.

Top Sirloin Steaks

Steak does work really well with sous vide, but where it really shines for me is on these normally kind of tough cuts that are usually cheaper at the store. Top sirloin is usually a great bargain compared to rib eyes, filets, and strips. In this recipe I will also show how you can get a little smoke flavor in before you finish them up with the sear. That step is not necessary, but a great option if you like a little smoke on your steak.

Prep time: 10 minutes **Cook Time:** 6 hours 10 minutes **Serves:** 6

Ingredients
1 whole top sirloin steak cut into singles
2 tbs FreshJax Camp Fire Sea Salt
2 tbs FreshJax course ground pepper
1 tbs FreshJax Garlic Herb Blend
Duck Fat Spray (or any other spray oil)

Directions

Turn your pellet grill on low smoke or start your grill with a small fire with some smoking wood or use a smoke tube with pellets. Keep the temperature under 160f/71.11c

Place the steaks on the smoker for 15 minutes then remove.

Pre-heat the sous vide bath to 130f/54.44c

Season the steaks with half of the rub and place in the vacuum bag and seal.

Cook in the bath for 6 hours

Remove steaks from the bag and pat them dry. Season with the remaining rub.

Heat the grill back up to over 500f/260c before putting the steaks on.

Spray the duck fat on the steaks. Place the steaks on and sear for about 30 seconds on each side. Flip them a couple times until you get a decent sear color.

Remove from the grill and let rest for a couple minutes.

Serve and enjoy!

Lamb Recipes

Roasts, Ribs, Chops, and More!

Greek Style Domestic Leg of Lamb

I have never been a lover of imported lamb. To me, the 100% grass fed stuff from Australia and New Zealand is way to gamey for me and when I tried to make some for my family, they almost spit it out. But when I am able to get some domestic lamb, now that is awesome. Domestic lamb is usually grain finished, just like most beef we are used to. It is hard to find in your local store, but online sources such as Porter Road and Crowd Cow makes it easy to get some shipped right to your door. Order some domestic lamb and give this recipe a try if you never thought you liked lamb!

Prep time: 20 minutes **Cook Time:** 7 hours **Serves:** 6-8

Ingredients
1 bone-in Domestic leg of lamb
2 tbs FreshJax Mesquite Lime Sea Salt
1 tbs FreshJax Citrus Pepper Blend
4 tbs FreshJax Greek Seasoning

Directions
Pre heat sous vide bath to 140f/60c

Season the lamb with half the rub then seal in the vacuum bag.

Cook in the sous vide bath for 6 hours

Pre-heat your smoker to 275f/135c and use some pecan or apple wood.

Place bag with lamb in an ice bath for 30 minutes while the smoker heats up.

Remove lamb from the bag, leave it wet, season with the FreshJax Greek Seasoning.

Smoke for 35 minutes to one hour or until the internal temperature reaches 140f/60c again.

If Possible, use a rotisserie for a more uniform bark!

Remove from smoker and serve!

Lamb Spareribs

One thing I can say about lamb ribs is they are much fattier than I thought they would be. As I have said before my family are not big lamb eaters, but I really like domestic lamb when I can get ahold of it. These are actually fantastic but just be aware they will flare up on the grill! Make sure to trim most of the fat cap off of these also. I Basted these with "The Farm Sauce" which is very savory and has a horseradish kick. www.thefarmsauce.com

Prep time: 10 minutes **Cook Time:** 25 hours **Serves:** 4

Ingredients
2 racks of Domestic Lamb Ribs

Rub
2 tbs FreshJax Mesquite Lime salt
1 tbs FreshJax Lemon zest
1 tbs FreshJax Orange zest
1 tbs FreshJax Course Ground Pepper
2 tbs FreshJax Garlic Herb Blend

Directions
Pre-heat the sous vide bath to 140f/60c

Season the ribs with half the rub.

Bag the ribs in the vacuum bag and seal. Place in the bath for 24 hours.

Pre-heat your grill to 400f/204cc

Remove the ribs from the sous vide, then remove from the bag and keep wet. Add the remaining seasoning to the ribs.

Place on the grill and cook over direct flame. Be careful as they will flare up!

Baste with The Farm Sauce during cooking

Remove from the grill and rest for 5 minutes.

Slice up serve and enjoy!

Sous Vide and Seared Rack of Lamb

Rack of lamb is probably the most popular cuts next to leg of lamb. Although it still has a bit of a fat cap, the meat is mostly lean and flavorful. I do not usually take the time to French the bones but to each his own. This rub was the same as I used on the lam T-bones I cooked at the same time and both were delicious! I used the domestic lamb from Porter Road online butchers here https://shrsl.com/2k4o8

Prep time: 15 minutes **Cook Time:** 4 hours 15 minutes **Serves:** 6

Ingredients
1 Domestic lamb Rack

Rub
2 tbs FreshJax Rosemary lemon sea slat
1 tsp FreshJax Lemon zest
1 tsp FreshJax Orange zest
1 tbs FreshJax Course Ground Pepper
1 tbs FreshJax Garlic powder
1 tbs FreshJax Onion powder
2 tsp FreshJax Thyme
1 tsp FreshJax ground cardamom
1 tsp FreshJax ground cumin

Directions
Pre-heat the sous vide bath to 138f/58.88c

Season the roast with half the rub.

Bag the roast in the vacuum bag and seal. Place in the bath for 4 hours.

Pre-heat your grill to 400f/204c

Remove the roast from the sous vide and the bag and pat dry. Add the remaining seasoning.

Place on the grill and cook over direct heat.

Grill until you get a nice crust.

Remove from the grill and rest for 5 minutes.

Slice up serve and enjoy!

Seared Lamb T-Bones

Also known a loin chops, these are kind of small, but tasty! They are already mostly tender, so you do not need a long time on these at all. Be cautious when searing to not overcook them as they don't need much. Tender, juicy, and awesome! I used the same rub, cooking time, and searing as I did the lamb rack. I used the domestic lamb from Porter Road online butchers here https://shrsl.com/2k4o8

Prep time: 5 minutes **Cook Time:** 4 hours 5 minutes **Serves:** 3

Ingredients

6 Domestic lamb T-bones (loin chops)

Rub

2 tbs FreshJax Rosemary lemon sea slat
1 tsp FreshJax Lemon zest
1 tsp FreshJax Orange zest
1 tbs FreshJax Course Ground Pepper
1 tbs FreshJax Garlic powder
1 tbs FreshJax Onion powder
2 tsp FreshJax Thyme
1 tsp FreshJax ground cardamom
1 tsp FreshJax ground cumin

Directions

Pre-heat the sous vide bath to 138f/58.88c

Season the roast with half the rub.

Bag the roast in the vacuum bag and seal. Place in the bath for 4 hours.

Pre-heat your grill to 400f/204c

Remove the roast from the sous vide and the bag and pat dry. Add the remaining seasoning.

Place on the grill and cook over direct heat.

Grill until you get a nice crust.

Remove from the grill and rest for 5 minutes.

Slice up serve and enjoy!

Smoked Lamb Shoulder

Lamb shoulder is like most other shoulders, it is usually tough, well marbled, and has a bone in it. This recipe is kind or more like a traditional smoked mutton from the West-Central Kentucky area. Usually this is cooked well done like most other shoulders but using sous vide we can make it more of a medium-well so we can render some fat without overcooking it. Trim as much surface fat as possible. I used the domestic lamb from Porter Road online butchers here - https://shrsl.com/2k4o8

Prep time: 15 minutes **Cook Time:** 26 hours **Serves:** 6

Ingredients
2 Domestic lamb shoulders

Rub
2 tbs FreshJax Cherry Wood Smoked salt
1 tsp FreshJax Lemon zest
1 tbs FreshJax Course Ground Pepper
1 tbs FreshJax Garlic powder
1 tbs FreshJax Onion powder
2 tsp FreshJax ground rosemary
2 tsp FreshJax Thyme

Directions
Pre-heat the sous vide bath to 148f/64.44c

Season the roast with half the rub. Bag the roast in the vacuum bag and seal.

Place in the bath for 24 hours.

Pre-heat your grill to 275f/135cc

Remove the roast from the sous vide and place in an ice bath for 30 minutes. remove from the bag and keep wet. Add the remaining seasoning.

Place on the grill and cook over indirect heat with some cherry wood.

Make sure you monitor the internal temperature, so you do not go over the 148f you cooked it to in the bath.

Remove from the grill and rest for 5 minutes.

Slice up serve and enjoy!

Lamb & Beef Gyro Kabobs

This is a great recipe to change things up and it is very easy. I used a mixture for 2 to 1 ground beef with ground lamb and it worked great. You could do this with all lamb or all beef as well. These are great to make ahead of time also and keep refrigerated and just sear them up and eat.

Prep time: 20 minutes **Cook Time:** 3 hours **Serves:** 6

Ingredients

1 lb ground domestic lamb
2 lbs ground 80/20 beef
1/2 cup breadcrumbs
1/4 cup onions chopped fine
2 eggs
3 tbs FreshJax Greek Seasoning
1 tbs FreshJax Garlic Herb Blend
1 tbs FreshJax course black pepper
2 tsp FreshJax ground cumin
2 tsp FreshJax ground coriander

Directions

Pre-heat the sous vide bath to 140f/60c

Mix the lamb, beef, breadcrumbs, eggs, onions, and 2/3rds of the seasonings.

Form the meat into 1/8 lb cylinders and place on skewers

Make sure the meat covers the pointed end of the skewer and vacuum seal.

Place bags in the sous vide bath and cook for 2 hours.

Pre-heat grill to 400f/204c for searing.

Remove skewers from bag and pat dry. Season with the remaining seasoning.

Grill over direct heat to sear.

Remove from grill and skewers, and slice into smaller pieces.

Serve on warm pita bread with tzatziki sauce, lettuce, tomato, feta cheese, onion, etc.

Pork Recipes

Roasts, Ribs, Chops, and More!

Bacon Wrapped Pork Tenderloin

One of the things that I hate the most when trying to make something stuffed or wrapped in bacon when I cook traditionally, is trying to get the interior cooked perfect while getting the outside crispy. I like to cook my pork tenderloin to the lower end of medium, around 145f/62.77c so if I just cooked this on the smoker, I would have to either settle for over cooked pork or under cooked bacon. So, besides producing a much moister tenderloin, I get crispy bacon on top of it!

Prep time: 45 minutes **Cook Time:** 2 hours 45 minutes **Serves:** 10-20

Ingredients

2 whole pork tenderloins
12 strips of bacon
1 tbs FreshJax Citrus Pepper
1 tbs FreshJax Mesquite Lime Sea salt
3 tbs FreshJax Rosy Cheeks BBQ Rub
1 cup of the BBQ sauce of your choice

Directions

Pre-heat the sous vide bath to 145f/62.77c

Remove the pork tenderloins from the package. Season with half of the citrus pepper and mesquite lime salt.

Make a bacon weave with the bacon strips. It is easy to do, search YouTube if you need a video for how to.

Season the side of the bacon weave facing you with the rest of the citrus pepper, mesquite lime salt, and half of the Rosy Cheeks rub. Wrap the bacon around the tenderloins and flip it over. Season the outside of the bacon with the rest of the Rosy Cheeks BBQ rub. Vacuum the pork and cook for 4-5 hours.

Pre-heat the smoker to 350f/176.66c and add a piece of pecan or cherry wood.

Remove the pork from the bag, leave it wet, add a little more of the rub and place on the smoker.

After about 30 minutes baste the pork with the BBQ sauce. Cook for another 10-15 minutes.

Remove from the smoker and serve!

Fire & Water Cooking

Pulled Pork Carnitas

This is another great recipe that can be used and converted to many different finishes. Carnitas are pork taco's in case you did not know, and they are usually done with roasted or pulled pork shoulder or Boston butt. The cooking process can be used for several other pork roast recipes including traditional barbecue pulled pork, Cuban mojo roast pork, or a million others. Be sure to trim as much surface fat as possible to get a better bark. Being able to re-incorporate the juices from the bag makes the pork super moist! Since I am making Carnitas, you can serve them on tortillas with all the taco fixings including guacamole, sour cream, shredded cheese, lettuce, salsa, red onions, tomatoes, and much more.

Prep time: 45 minutes **Cook Time:** 38 hours **Serves:** 10-15

Ingredients

1 bone-in or boneless pork shoulder or Boston butt 5-7lbs
2 tbs FreshJax Mesquite Lime Sea Salt
4 tbs FreshJax Taco Seasoning
2 tbs FreshJax Citrus Pepper seasoning
1 tbs FreshJax Peppered Habanero seasoning (optional)

Directions

Pre heat sous vide bath to 150f/65.55c

Season the pork with the FreshJax Mesquite lime Sea Salt rub or kosher salt, then seal in the vacuum bag.

Cook in the sous vide bath for 36-48 hours

Pre-heat your smoker to 275f/135c and use some pecan or apple wood. Place bag with pork in an ice bath for 45 minutes while the smoker heats up.

Remove pork from the bag, reserve the bag juices to use later after you pull it. leave it wet, season with the FreshJax Taco Seasoning, the citrus pepper, and the Peppered Habanero.

Smoke with a lighter wood like apple or peach for 45 minutes to one hour or until the internal temperature reaches 150f/66cc or you have a nice bark.

Remove the pork from the smoker, let I rest in a pan until you are ready to pull it. Pull the pork and pour some of the reserved bag juices back in.

Serve with tortillas and all the accompaniments!

Porchetta

This is one of my most favorite things to do with pork belly by far. The best way to finish it for me is with a rotisserie, but I know not everyone has one. You can also finish it cooking direct heat at a and turn it every 5 minutes or so until it gets a good crust. Sous vide allows you to cook it completely and make sure it is super tender before putting in on the grill. This is a very rich and flavorful recipe for sure. I use skinless pork belly as there are more steps involved with skin on.

Prep time: 45 minutes **Cook Time:** 25 hours **Serves:** 8-10

Ingredients

- 3-5 lb skinless pork belly
- 2 ½ tbs FreshJax Rosemary Lemon Sea salt
- 2 tbs FreshJax Citrus Pepper
- 2 tbs FreshJax Garlic Herb blend
- 1 tbs FreshJax ground thyme
- 1 tbs FreshJax ground rosemary
- 1 tbs FreshJax ground sage
- 1/3 cup olive oil
- Butcher's twine to tie it up

Directions

Pre-heat the sous vide bath to 165f/73.88c

Score the pork belly into a diamond shape on the side without the fat, we will be rolling this up. Mix the about 2/3's of the seasoning with the olive oil to make a paste. Spread the paste all over the diamond cuts so it penetrates the meat.

Starting from one end, roll the pork belly into a tube. Use butcher's twine to secure it every 1 ½ inches.

Season the outside of the pork with half the remaining seasoning. Bag it up in the vacuum bag. Toss in the bath for 24 hours.

Pre-heat the smoker to 350f/176.66c and add some pecan wood.

Remove from the bag and add the last of the seasoning. Put on the rotisserie or the smoker.

Cook until the exterior is crispy and has a nice bark.

Remove from the smoker and slice into 1-inch slices. Serve and Enjoy!

St Louis Spareribs

I am one of those guys who does not like to sauce his ribs when I cook them most of the time, especially if I have company. I like to switch it up and use sauce as a condiment and put it on after and allow my guests to choose which flavors they like also. Sous vide works amazing on ribs and you get to avoid the "wrapping" stage that most do to make them tender.

Prep time: 15 minutes **Cook Time:** 38 hours **Serves:** 6-8

Ingredients

2 racks St Louis Cut Spareribs

Rub

4 tbs FreshJax Rosy Cheeks BBQ Rub
1 tbs FreshJax Mesquite Lime Sea Salt
1 tbs FreshJax Cherry Wood Smoked Sea Salt
2 tbs FreshJax Garlic Herb blend

Directions

Pre-heat the sous vide bath to 150f/65.55c

Remove the membrane from the back of the rib racks.

I do not use a "binder" for my ribs except water, but you are welcome to use what you like. Season the ribs with half the rub.

Bag the ribs in the expandable vacuum bags and seal. Place in the bath for 36 hours.

Pre-heat your smoker to 250f/121.11c and add some pecan and cherry wood.

Remove the ribs from the sous vide and place in an ice bath for 30 minutes or so.

Remove the ribs from the bag and keep wet. Add the remaining seasoning to the ribs.

Place on the smoker and let them cook until they get a nice bark. You can spritz them water or apple juice after the first 20 minutes to help develop more smoke and bark.

If you like you can add barbecue sauce in the last ten minutes to glaze them.

Remove from the smoker and rest for 5 minutes.

Slice up serve and enjoy!

Jamaican Jerk Pork Tenderloin

Here is another great Jerk recipe that is super easy and very versatile! If you like a little spice, you can add a little more of the jerk seasoning. The pork tenderloin will be nice and medium and super juicy. You can do a little lower temperature if you like your pork a little pinker. I usually finish it with a fruit-based finishing glaze to have a more of a "Sweet Heat". You can use this Jerk Seasoning for ribs, pork loin, and other cuts as well.

Prep time: 15 minutes **Cook Time:** 3 hours 10 minutes **Serves:** 6

Ingredients

2 whole Pork tenderloins
1 tbs FreshJax Rosemary Lemon Sea Salt
3 tbs FreshJax Island Spice Jerk Seasoning
Duck Fat Spray or other spray oil

Directions

Pre-heat the sous vide bath to 148f/64.44c

Season the pork with half of the seasonings.

Bag it up, vacuum seal, and toss it in the bath for 3 hours

Heat up your charcoal grill until the coals are whited over with ash. Make sure the grates are at least 4 inches from the coals, so you get a nice sear. If you like you can add some apple or cherry wood chips to the fire for a little bit of smoke.

Remove the pork from the bag and pat it dry.

Spray with the duck fat and add the rest of the seasoning.

Add the pork to the grill and flip it often. You do not want it to burn, but you do want it crispy with a little char to it.

Remove from the grill and serve with yellow rice, black beans, and a pineapple mango salsa or some other fruit sauce.

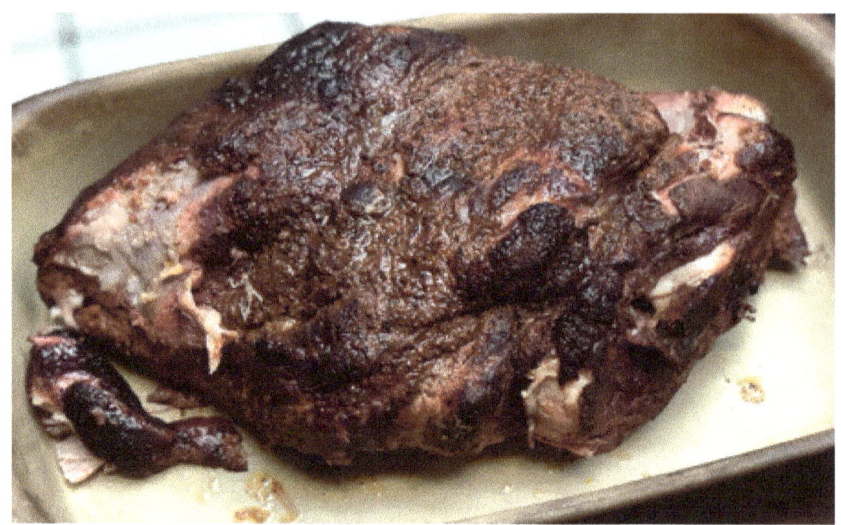

Pulled Pork Shoulder

This is my way of doing sous vide pulled pork that best represents the traditional way with some better results in my opinion. Try it this way and compare it yourself to your old way and see if I am right. It will be moister and less of a hassle but will take a little more time planning. I use Boston butt, but you could also use shoulder.

Prep time: 30 minutes **Cook Time:** 38 hours **Serves:** 6-8

Ingredients
1 5-7-pound pork butt
2 tbs FreshJax Mesquite Lime Sea Salt
3 tbs FreshJax Rosy Cheeks BBQ Rub
2 tbs FreshJax Smokey Southwest

Directions

Pre-heat the sous vide bath to 155f/68.33c

Trim most of the exterior fat from the pork butt. You will not need.

Season the pork with half of the seasonings. Bag it up, vacuum seal, and toss it in the bath for 36 hours. You may need to use the expandable vacuum bag for this.

When the time is up, place the pork butt into an ice bath for at least 1 hour to chill it down. If you have time, let it sit overnight in the fridge.

Pre-heat the smoker to 275f/135c and add some pecan wood.

Cut a hole in the bag and drain the juices into a bowl, the fat should stay in the bag. Remove the pork and put on a rack on a sheet pan. Leave the pork wet and apply the remaining seasoning.

Place on the smoker for one hour, spritzing it with water or apple juice after the first 30 minutes.

Remove the pork from the smoker after it develops a nice dark bark but do not let it go over the 155f/68.33c internal temperature you sous vide it to.

Place the pork in a pan and pull as usual. Add the reserved bag juices back into the pork and serve!

Pork Loin Roast

Pork loin roast is one of the best things you can use your sous vide for as they tend to dry out if cooked traditionally since they are so lean. This recipe will allow you to make some really tender, juicy, and flavorful pork to please your whole family! I like to finish them over an open flame or with a super-hot torch to get a little bit of char.

Prep time: 10 minutes **Cook Time:** 6 hours 10 minutes **Serves:** 6

Ingredients

1 3-4lb pork loin roast

Rub

1 tbs FreshJax Mesquite Lime Sea Salt
1 tbs FreshJax Cherry Wood Smoked Sea Salt
1 tbs FreshJax Garlic Herb blend
1 tbs FreshJax Citrus Pepper Blend

Directions

Pre-heat the sous vide bath to 148f/64.44c

Season the roast with half the rub.

Bag the pork loin and Place in the bath for 6 hours.

Pre-heat your grill to 500f/260c and add some pecan and cherry wood.

Remove loin from the sous vide and place in an ice bath for 5 minutes or so. We are not wanting to completely chill the interior as we will be quick searing it.

Remove the pork from the bag and pat it dry. Add the remaining seasoning.

Place on grill and sear on all sides. You want a little char but don't burn it!

If you like you can add barbecue sauce or another glaze to finish.

Slice up serve and enjoy!

Sous Vide Close Proximity Smoked Pork Chops

This is a trick I learned from my friend Meathead Goldwyn at AmazingRibs.com. It does require you have the GrillGrates brand grates, but if you have others you may be able to rig a way to do it anyway. The GrillGrates work so well due to the channel that is about 1/3 of an inch deep, it makes it easy to add smoking pellets in them when the grates are hot. You can use this trick on steak, chicken, or anything you want to grill and get some smoke on!

Prep time: 10 minutes **Cook Time:** 2 hours 10 minutes **Serves:** 4

Ingredients

4 large pork chops
1 tbs FreshJax Cherrywood Smoked Sea Salt
1 tbs FreshJax Citrus Pepper Blend
1 tbs FreshJax Garlic Herb Blend
1 tsp FreshJax Toasted Onion
Duck Fat Spray

Directions

Pre-heat the sous bath to 145f/62.77c

Season the pork chops with half the seasoning and vacuum seal. Add to the bath and cook for 2 hours.

Pre-heat your grill and place the GrillGrates directly over the hottest part of the fire with the grooves facing up.

Just before removing the pork chops from the sous vide, place a couple handfuls of smoking pellets in the grooves of the GrillGrates.

Remove the pork chops from the bag and pat dry. Spray with some duck fay spray of any spray oil.

Add some more of the seasoning and grill on both sides until you get some nice color and grill marks.

Remove from the grill and rest for a couple minutes before serving.

Poultry Recipes

Chicken, Turkey, Duck, and More!

Cherry Wood Smoked Chicken with Duck Fat

This recipe will showcase another great aspect of using the sous vide and smoker together. Cherry wood works really well with poultry as it gives the skin a great color and sweet flavor. Spatchcocking (removing the backbone and flattening) allows the chicken to cook more even and fit in the vacuum bag easier. Using the duck fat spray also give the bird a deep, rich flavor and helps with crisping. If you have not used Duck Fat Spray in your cooking, you need to give it a try! Find it in my Amazon Store.

Prep time: 30 minutes **Cook Time:** 5 hours **Serves:** 6

Ingredients
1 whole chicken
Duck Fat Spray (you can use any other spray oil)

Rub
2 tbs FreshJax Rosemary Lemon Sea Salt
2 tbs FreshJax Paprika
2 tbs FreshJax Garlic Herb blend
1 tbs FreshJax Citrus Pepper

Directions
Pre-heat the sous vide bath to 148f/64.44c

Remove the backbone of the chicken and flatten it out on a sheet pan.

Season the chicken with half of the rub and bag it up into the vacuum bag.

Place the sealed bag into the sous vide bath and cook for 4 hours.

Pre-heat the smoker to 400f/204c and use some cherry chunks for smoke.

Remove the chicken from the bag and place on a wire rack on a sheet pan. Pat the chicken dry, and then spray the chicken with a nice coat of the duck fat spray, then apply the rest of the seasoning rub.

Place chicken on the smoker on the wire rack, this makes it easier to remove when done.

Let cook on the smoker for 15-20 minutes then apply another coat of the duck fat spray and let cook for another 10 minutes or so until the skin is crispy.

Remove from the smoker and serve!

Caribbean Jerk Chicken

I have been to Jamaica twice in my life and have dined on jerk chicken many more times when visiting other Caribbean islands and in the states. Whenever I eat it, I feel like blasting some Bob Marley and drinking a Red Stripe Beer! Traditional jerk chicken is not smoked low and slow, but grilled hot and fast over charcoals, and is nice and spicy. Sous vide allows you to cook the meat all the way through before grilling it up for some crispy charred skin while keeping it nice and juicy. The FreshJax Island Spice worked amazing on this recipe!

Prep time: 20 minutes **Cook Time:** 5 hours **Serves:** 6

Ingredients
1 whole chicken cut into quarters skin on
1 tbs FreshJax Rosemary Lemon Sea Salt
3 tbs FreshJax Island Spice Jerk Seasoning
Duck Fat Spray or other spray oil

Directions
Pre-heat the sous vide bath to 148f/64.44c

Season the chicken with half of the seasonings. Bag it up, vacuum seal, and toss it in the bath for 4 hours

Heat up your charcoal grill until the coals are whited over with ash. Make sure the grates are at least 4 inches from the coals, so you get a nice char. If you like you can add some apple or cherry wood chips to the fire for a little bit of smoke.

Remove the chicken from the bag. You will want to pat it as dry as possible so the skin will get crispy.

Add the rest of the seasoning.

Spray with the duck fat or other spray oil.

Add the chicken to the grill and flip it often. You do not want it to burn, but you do want it crispy with a little char to it.

Remove from the grill and let it rest for 5 minutes.

Serve with white rice, black beans, and a Red Stripe Beer! Enjoy!

Whole Rotisserie Chicken

Cooking poultry whole like this requires you to take something else into consideration, the cavity. Sous vide uses water and conductive heat to cook food. So, a hunk of meat with a gaping, open, cavity filled with air is not a safe way to cook with this method as it will allow bacteria to grow. That is, unless we fill that cavity with liquid. This will allow the water bath to heat the liquid in the bag to the same cooking temperature allowing you to cook it safely. Add just enough chicken stock to fill the cavity. Use the pulse function on the vacuum sealer to seal the bag without suctioning the liquid. You can finish on the rotisserie or just in the smoker if you wish.

Prep time: 20 minutes **Cook Time:** 7 hours **Serves:** 6

Ingredients
1 whole chicken
2-3 cups of chicken stock

Rub
2 tbs FreshJax Rosemary Lemon Sea Salt
2 tbs FreshJax Garlic Herb Blend
1 tbs FreshJax Paprika
1 tbs FreshJax Citrus Pepper Blend

Directions
Pre-heat the sous vide bath to 148f/64.44c

Season the chicken with half of the seasonings. Add the chicken and the stock to a vacuum sealer bag. You may need to use the expandable vacuum bags. Seal using the pulse function.

Add the chicken to the sous vide bath and cook for 6 hours.

Preheat your smoker or grill to 375f/190.55c with a mix of cherry and pecan wood.

Remove chicken from the bag and season with the remaining rub.

Place on the grill or rotisserie and cook until the skin gets crispy, about 45 minutes.

Serve and enjoy!

Spatchcocked Turkey

Turkey is not just for the holidays! I have to admit thought, I do not even try to cook turkey whole using sous vide. Spatchcocked is the only way to go for me just for the matter of the size. You will need a larger container and the expandable vacuum sealer bags for sure on this one. I did go for a more "traditional" seasoning on this one, but as always you can use whatever seasoning you wish. Some people like to separate the white and dark meat and cook them at different temperatures, but I prefer to meet both in the middle and cook the whole thing at 148-150f. Pro Tip: when the turkey has been on the smoker for 20 minutes spray it with some Duck fat or any other spray oil.

Prep time: 30 minutes **Cook Time:** 9 hours **Serves:** 8-12

Ingredients
1 whole young turkey (15-16 lbs)

Rub
3 tbs FreshJax Rosemary Lemon Sea Salt
1 tbs FreshJax ground thyme
1 tbs FreshJax Sage
1 tbs FreshJax ground rosemary
2 tbs FreshJax Garlic Herb Blend
1 tbs FreshJax Paprika
1 tbs FreshJax Citrus Pepper Blend

Directions
Pre-heat the sous vide bath to 148f/64.44c

Remove the backbone and flatten out. Pin the wings back. Season with half the rub.

Place in the expanded vacuum bag and seal up. Place in the sous vide bath and cook for 8 hours.

Pre-heat the smoker to 375f/190.55c and add some apple wood.

Remove the turkey from the bag and add the rest of the seasoning. Place on the smoker for about 45 minutes until the skin is crisp.

Remove from the smoker, let rest for 10 minutes and serve.

Sous Vide Smoked Fried Chicken

Yeah, I know, a three-step process for fried chicken? Well, I suggest you try it at least once to see for yourself. You can skip the smoking part if you like, but the sous vide bath will make sure you have super moist, thoroughly cooked fried chicken! No more dried out white meat! The smoking will add another layer of flavor for sure.

Prep time: 40 minutes **Cook Time:** 5 hours **Serves:** 6

Ingredients
1 whole chicken quartered
3 cups all-purpose flour
2 eggs
4 tbs water
2 tbs FreshJax Rosemary Lemon Sea Salt
2 tbs FreshJax black pepper
2 tbs FreshJax Bold Bayou Cajun
2 quarts vegetable oil

Directions
Pre-heat the smoker to 180f/82.22c and use some with apple wood

Season the chicken with salt and pepper and place on the smoker for about 20 minutes.

Pre-heat the sous vide bath to 148f/64.44c

Let the chicken cool for 10 minutes then bag it in the vacuum bag.

Place the chicken in the sous vide bath for 4 hours.

Remove from the bath and chill in an ice bath while you heat the oil to 375f/190.55c

Mix the seasonings with the flour. Make an egg wash with the eggs and water.

Remove the chicken from the bag and dip in the flour, then the egg, and then the flour again. Shake off the excess flour and place in the oil.

Fry until they are golden brown.

Let rest on paper towels to drain the oil.

serve and enjoy!

Alabama Style BBQ Chicken

I grew up in Upstate New York where we had Cornell Chicken for out summer cook outs. The marinade for that chicken is very similar to this Alabama Style White Barbecue Sauce. I got most of the ingredients from AmazingRibs.com as they have many base sauce recipes on there. This is great on chicken, but I put it on everything. It is also fantastic on pulled pork!

Prep time: 30 minutes **Cook Time:** 5 hours **Serves:** 6

Ingredients
1 whole chicken cut into quarters skin on
2 tbs FreshJax Rosemary Lemon Sea Salt
2 tbs FreshJax Garlic Herb blend
1 tbs FreshJax Paprika
1 tbs FreshJax Onion powder
1 tbs FreshJax Citrus Pepper

The Sauce
2 cups Dukes Mayonnaise
1/3 cup apple cider vinegar
3 tbs lemon juice
2 tbs Garlic powder
2 tsp powdered mustard
2 tbs prepared horseradish
2 tbs course ground black pepper
1 tsp cayenne pepper

Directions
Pre-heat the sous vide bath to 148f/64.44c

Season the chicken with half the rub and bag it up in a vacuum sealed bag.

Drop the chicken in the bath and cook for 4 hours.

Mix all the ingredients for the sauce and let it sit as the chicken cooks. It is better the longer it sits.

Heat the smoker up to about 350f/176.6c with some pecan wood.

Remove the chicken from the bag and add the remaining seasoning to the chicken.

Place the chicken in the smoker for 45 minutes or until the skin is crispy.

Remove the chicken from the smoker and serve with the sauce.

Smoked Turkey Breast

For this turkey, I like to do a simpler type rub and treat it like they do in Texas. You can finish it on the regular smoker or on a rotisserie if you have one. Sous vide allows you to produce a very moist and tender bird without having to worry about injections and over brining. I use just a small amount of pecan or apple wood as to not over smoke it.

Prep time: 10 minutes **Cook Time:** 7 hours **Serves:** 8

Ingredients
1 young turkey breast
Duck fat spray or other spray oil

Rub
3 tbs FreshJax Rosemary Lemon Sea Salt
3 tbs FreshJax Garlic Herb Blend
1 tbs FreshJax Onion powder
1 tbs FreshJax Citrus Pepper Blend

Directions
Pre-heat the sous vide bath to 148f/64.44c

Season the breast with half the rub.

Place in the expanded vacuum bag and seal up. Place in the sous vide bath and cook for 6 hours.

Pre-heat the smoker to 375f/190.55c and add some pecan wood.

Remove the turkey from the bag and dry the skin off with paper towels. Spray with some of the duck fat and add the rest of the seasoning.

Place on the smoker for about 45 minutes until the skin is crisp.

After 20 minutes spray with some more duck fat.

Remove from the smoker, let rest for 10 minutes and serve.

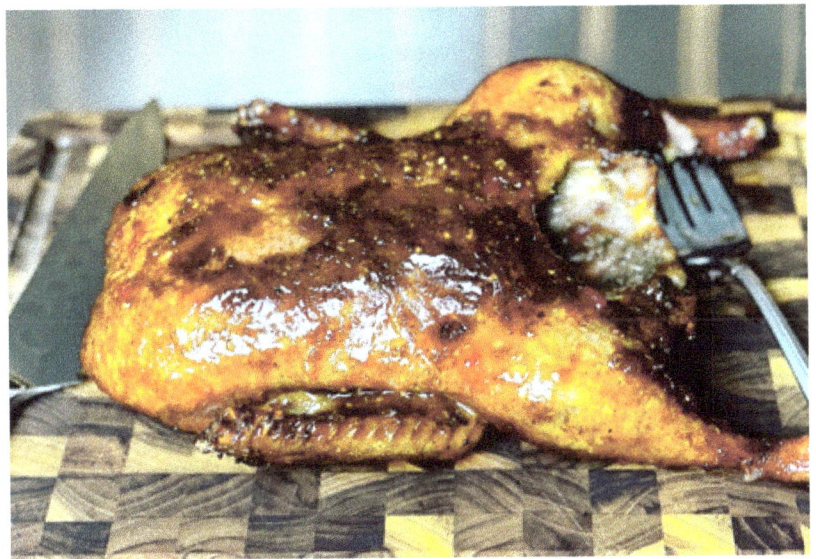

Sous Vide and Smoked Whole Duck

If you have never cooked a whole duck before, this is one you need to try. Sous vide makes sure this gets cooked all the wat through, does not dry out, and makes sure to render a good amount of the fat before putting on the smoker to finish the skin. You can avoid having to use the stock in the bag if you spatchcock it instead of keeping whole. You can also use the orange sauce package if yours comes with it or you can use Frank's Sweet Chili Sauce as a glaze at the end.

Prep time: 20 minutes **Cook Time:** 8 hours **Serves:** 4

Ingredients

1 whole duck
2 cups chicken stock (if whole)

Rub

2 tbs FreshJax Rosemary Lemon Sea Salt
1 tbs FreshJax Paprika
1 tbs FreshJax Garlic Herb blend
1 tbs FreshJax Citrus Pepper
1 tbs FreshJax Allspice
1 tbs FreshJax Ginger
1 tbs FreshJax Orange Peel powder
¼ cup Frank's Sweet Chili sauce

Directions

Pre-heat the sous vide bath to 150f/65.55c

Trim any extra fat and skin from the duck. Season the duck with half the rub.

Add the duck to the bag and then the stock. If you are spatchcocking the duck no need for the stock. Place in the bath and cook for 7 hours.

Pre-heat the smoker to 325F/162.77c

Remove the duck from the bag and place on a rack on top of a sheet pan. Season with the rest of the seasoning. Place on smoker for 20 minutes or so.

When the skin starts to get golden brown, baste with the Sauce for a nice glaze. Let the glaze get nice and tacky before removing.

Remove from the smoker and serve!

Seafood Recipes

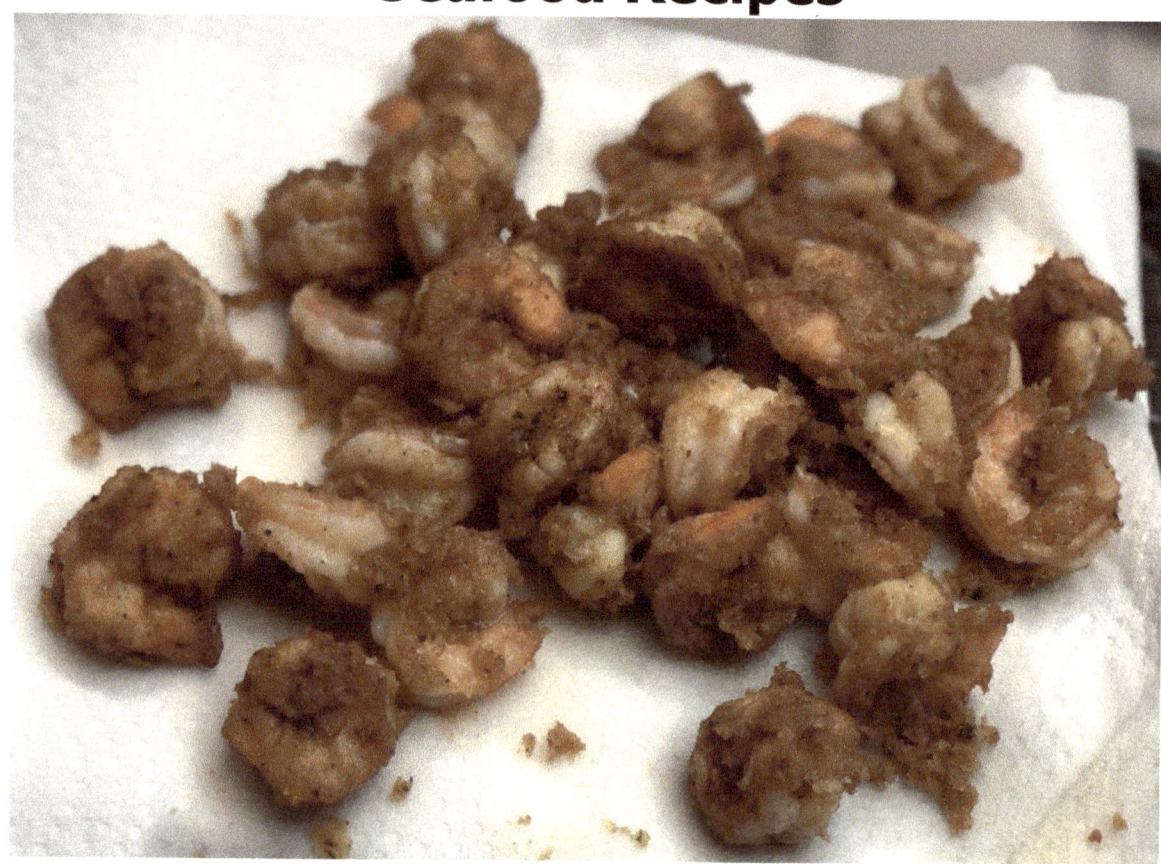

Fish and shellfish

Seared Wild Alaskan Cod

We do not eat enough fish on my family for some reason. It probably has more to do with a lack of available fresh fish at decent prices, whenever I do cook it, we love it. I got these cod filets from Wild Alaskan Company along with some amazing salmon. This is a simple recipe and will really shine with freshest cod you can get. Look them up and give them a try!

Prep time: 10 minutes **Cook Time:** 1 hour **Serves:** 6

Ingredients

4-6 pieces of wild caught Alaskan cod
Duck Fat Spray or other spray oil
1 tbs FreshJax rosemary lemon sea salt
1 tbs FreshJax Citrus pepper
1 tbs FreshJax Garlic Herb blend
½ of a fresh lemon

Directions

Pre-heat the sous vide bath to 134f/56.66c

Season the fish with half of the seasonings. Place in the vacuum bag and seal.

Place the fish in the sous vide bath and cook for 40 minutes. If the fish is frozen add another 10 minutes or so.

Pre-heat your grill to 500f/260c, I prefer a flat surface for this like a griddle.

Remove the fish from the bag and spray with a little duck fat spray or other spray oil.

Add the remaining seasoning to both sides of the fish.

Sear on each side for about 45 seconds or until you get a nice color. Squeeze the lemon over the fish to add a little acid.

Remove from the grill and serve!

Smoked Salmon

Salmon is the fish we eat most often in my house and sous vide works perfect with it. I lightly season it in the bag and a little after and then put it in the grill with a little smoke briefly to finish it up. I do not usually eat the skin, but you could crisp the skin if you wish. I finished this with a wasabi pesto sauce I purchased from the Amazon.

Prep time: 5 minutes **Cook Time:** 50 minutes **Serves:** 4-6

Ingredients

1 whole salmon filet cut into portions
2 tbs FreshJax Fresh Bay Seafood seasoning
1 tbs FreshJax Rosemary Lemon Sea Salt
1 tbs olive oil

Directions

Pre-heat the sous vide bath to 128f/53.33c

Coat the salmon with the olive oil and season with half of the rub. Place in the vacuum sealer bag and seal.

Place the salmon in the bath and cook for 40 minutes.

Pre-heat the grill to 400f/204c and add some apple wood chips.

Remove the fish from the bag, be careful as it will be easy to break apart. Pat it dry as much as possible

Add the remaining seasoning to the fish.

Place the fish on a rack and then on the grill for 10 minutes max. You just want to get a nice crust, do not burn it. You could also finish in a broiler or hit it with a torch.

Remove from the heat, serve with your favorite sauce!

Seared Tuna Steaks

I love sear tuna steaks! When I see them on sale, I buy them every time. This is a rather simple recipe but will turn out fantastic every single time. Be careful when removing from the bag and searing to not let them fall apart on you. Use a fish spatula if you have one. You can add some of the remaining marinade to a ½ cup of mayonnaise to make a nice dipping sauce.

Prep time: 10 minutes **Cook Time:** 1 hour 10 minutes **Serves:** 6-8

Ingredients

4 pieces of tuna steak
Duck Fat Spray or other spray oil

Marinade

½ cup of soy sauce
2 tbs honey
1 tbs FreshJax ground ginger
1 tbs FreshJax Garlic Herb Blend
1 tsp FreshJax ground all-spice

Directions

Pre-heat the sous vide bath to 115f/46.11c

Prepare the marinade and add to a dish that you can lay the tuna steaks in to soak. Let the tuna marinade for about 15 minutes on each side.

Place the tuna steaks in the vacuum bags with about 2 tablespoons of the marinade.

Place the fish in the sous vide bath and cook for 1 hour.

Pre-heat your grill to 500f/260c, I prefer a flat surface for this like a griddle.

Remove the fish from the bag and spray with a little duck fat spray or other spray oil.

Sear on each side for about 10 seconds or until you get a nice color.

Remove from the grill and serve!

Seared Scallops

Scallops are really a great seafood to use sous vide with as they are full of moisture but easy to dry out cooking traditionally and they can turn rubbery fast. You can sear them off in a pan, griddle, or any other flat cooking surface with a hot temperature. Simple seasoning is best to let them speak for themselves. Make sure to dry them completely when searing.

Prep time: 5 minutes **Cook Time:** 35 minutes **Serves:** 4

Ingredients

1 lb fresh seas scallops
Duck Fat Spray or other spray oil
1 tbs FreshJax rosemary lemon sea salt
1/2 tbs FreshJax Citrus pepper
1/2 tbs FreshJax Garlic Herb blend
½ of a fresh lemon

Directions

Pre-heat the sous vide bath to 126f/52.22

Season the scallops with half of the seasonings. Place in the vacuum bag and seal.

Place the scallops in the sous vide bath and cook for 30 minutes.

Pre-heat your grill to 500f/260c, I prefer a flat surface for this like a griddle.

Remove them from the bag, dry with paper towels completely.

Spray with a little duck fat spray or other spray oil.

Add the remaining seasoning to both sides of the scallops.

Sear on each side for about 45 seconds or until you get a nice color.

Squeeze the lemon over the top to add a little acid.

Remove from the grill and serve!

Pineapple Habanero Bacon Wrapped Shrimp Skewers

Although sous vide is not needed to make either the bacon or shrimp tender, it can do wonders for keeping the shrimp moist and not rubbery and getting the bacon par-cooked making it easier to crisp up. I used a great roasted Pineapple Habanero glaze from Terrapin Ridge Farms on Amazon you can find Here- https://amzn.to/3kmyGdb

Prep time: 40 minutes **Cook Time:** 2 hours **Serves:** 4

Ingredients
2 pounds medium to large deveined shrimp
1 pound of thin sliced bacon
½ cup Pineapple Habanero Glaze
1 tbs FreshJax Habanero Lime Salt
1 tbs FreshJax Citrus Pepper
1 tbs FreshJax Garlic Herb Blend

Directions
Pre heat water bath to 150f/65.55c

Vacuum seal the pack of bacon to make sure it does not leak, put in the bath for 1 hour to par cook.

Peel and remove the tails from the shrimp.

Remove the bacon from the bath and let cool a couple minutes. Season the shrimp with half the seasoning.

Wrap the shrimp with the bacon and place on the skewers. When done, add the remaining seasoning to the skewers.

Vacuum seal the skewers but make sure the point is covered. Sous vide for 15 minutes

Heat your grill up to 450f/232.22c

Remove the skewers from the bag and place on the grill. Baste the shrimp with the pineapple habanero glaze until they get nice and crispy.

Remove from the grill and serve!

Vegetable Based Recipes

Tofu, Cauliflower, Portobello, etc.

Tofu Barbecue Burnt Ends

So, why not tofu burnt ends? I have seen them made out of different kinds of meat from pork belly, chuck roast, and even hot dogs, so I think this is a great option for those on a meatless diet. We use the sous vide to cook the tofu down some and release some moisture before smoking it with some great barbecue flavors.

Prep time: 10 minutes **Cook Time:** 2 hours **Serves:** 6-8

Ingredients
1 package of firm tofu
1 tbs FreshJax Mesquite Lime Sea Salt
1 tbs FreshJax Citrus Pepper Blend
2 tbs FreshJax Rosy Cheeks barbecue rub
1 cup barbecue sauce

Directions
Pre heat sous vide bath to 158f/70c

Drain the tofu block and cut into 6 pieces about 1 1/2" thick. Place on sheet pan with paper towels and try and get a good amount of moisture out.

Season the tofu with half for the seasoning and bag it up into the vacuum bag. Be careful not to use too high a vacuum pressure so you do not squeeze it out of shape.
Cook for 2 hours in the bath.

Pre-heat your smoker to 275f/135c with some apple wood

Remove tofu from the bag and pat dry. Season with remaining rub. Place on the smoker for 15 minutes.

Remove from the smoker and cut into 2-inch cubes and toss in the barbecue sauce. Place the tofu on a rack on the smoker for another 10-15 minutes until the sauce glazes over.

Remove from smoker and serve!

Fire & Water Cooking

Black Bean Burger

Who doesn't love a good burger? Even those who are not on a meatless diet will love this awesome tasting burger! Sous vide lets it remain moist and juicy while the grill gives it the Smokey finish, we love. Make a big batch and freeze them for later to heat and eat.

Prep time: 40 minutes **Cook Time:** 2 hours **Serves:** 4

Ingredients

2 cans black beans drained and rinsed
1 cup finely chopped onion
½ cup finely chopped red pepper
½ cup feta cheese
¾ cup breadcrumbs
3 tbs mayonnaise
1 egg
¼ cup vegetable stock
2 tbs canola oil
2 tbs FreshJax Grill Master Blend
1 tbs FreshJax Garlic Herb Blend
1 tbs FreshJax Habanero Lime Salt
1 tbs FreshJax Citrus Pepper

Directions

Pre heat oven to 350f/176.66c

Spread the beans on a sheet pan in a single layer and place in the oven to dry them out for at least 30 minutes.

Add the oil to a pan and sweat the onions and peppers while the beans dry.

Pre-heat sous vide bath to 148f/64.44c

Add the beans and all other ingredients except 1 tablespoon of the Grill Master Blend into a food processor and pulse a few times to mix it up into a rough chop.

It should be able to make a good patty, if it is too dry you can add a little water to pulse again. Make into serving size patties.

Bag them up into a Ziploc bag or use the pulse function on the vacuum sealer being careful not to misshape them. Add to the bath and cook for 1 hour and 15 minutes.

Remove from the bag and season with the remaining Grill Master Blend.

Finish them on the grill over direct heat or finish in a pan on the stove.

Add cheese and the condiments of your choice.

Fire & Water Cooking

Cauliflower Sous Vide Steak

This recipe is not meant to simulate a real beef steak but is more of a different way to eat some great fresh vegetables. Sous vide will let you make this nice and tender before you put a nice sear on it. You can also change the marinade up a lot to your own personal taste. I made this a little spicy so you can add more or reduce the heat if you wish.

Prep time: 20 minutes **Cook Time:** 1 hour 10 minutes **Serves:** 3

Ingredients

1 large Cauliflower cut into 3 large pieces
1 tbs Balsamic Vinegar
1/2 cup vegetable stock
3 tbs olive oil
2 tbs FreshJax Grill Master Blend
1 tbs FreshJax Garlic Herb Blend
1 tbs FreshJax Smokey Southwest
1 tbs FreshJax Siracha Sea Salt
1 tbs FreshJax Citrus Pepper
Spray oil

Directions

Pre heat sous vide bath to 182f/83.33c

Mix all ingredients except the cauliflower in a bowl and whisk together

Add the cauliflower into vacuum sealer bags and add the marinade in each bag, just enough to cover the cauliflower and seal.

Place in the sous vide bath and cook for one hour.

Pre-heat your grill or pan up to 500f/260c

Remove from the sous vide and pat dry.

Add a little more of the FreshJax Grill Master if you wish.

Spray with a little spray oil and sear on the grill.

Remove from the heat and serve.

Grilled Portobello Mushrooms with Grilled Onions

Mushrooms pack an Umami punch, and this recipe doubles up on the umami. You can omit the onions if you wish and you can make this into a sandwich very easy. The mushrooms will absorb a lot of the marinade so be careful not to over season. If you have a set of GrillGrate brand grates, you can add some pellets to the grooves to do some close proximity smoking as seen on page 25 of this book.

Prep time: 20 minutes **Cook Time:** 1 hour 10 minutes **Serves:** 4

Ingredients

4 large portobello mushrooms
1 medium onion sliced thin
¼ cup red wine
2 tbs butter
4 tbs Worcestershire sauce
1 tbs red boat fish sauce (optional)
1/2 cup vegetable stock
2 tbs olive oil
2 tbs FreshJax Campfire sea salt
1 tbs FreshJax Thyme
1 tbs FreshJax Garlic Herb Blend
1 tbs FreshJax Citrus Pepper
Spray oil

Directions

Pre heat sous vide bath to 158f/70c

Mix the stock, Worcestershire, fish sauce, oil, and seasonings into a bowl and whisk.

Clean the mushrooms and remove the stalks if any. Add to vacuum bag with the marinade.

Place in the sous vide bath and cook for one hour. These will want to float so use a rack.

Pre-heat your grill or pan up to 500f/260c

In a pan add the butter, onions, red wine, and salt & pepper to taste. Cook the onions until they are brown then add the wine and reduce.

Remove mushrooms from the sous vide and pat dry.

Hit them with a little spray oil and sprinkle with salt and pepper. Add to grill and get a nice char.

Remove from the heat and serve with the onions on top.

Sous Vide and Smoked Blue Cheese Slaw

I have to admit this recipe took me by surprise! I had seen a few different ways to incorporate some to whole cabbage before, but never like this. I got this idea by mixing the best of all the videos I found on this. I cored a whole cabbage, cooked it sous vide with some butter and spices, then added some seasoned blue cheese dressing and smoked it! It is fantastic even if you do not like cabbage!

Prep time: 15 minutes **Cook Time:** 1 hour 45 minutes **Serves:** 6

Ingredients
1 large Cabbage cored
¾ stick of butter room temperature
2 tbs FreshJax Garlic Herb Blend
2 tbs FreshJax Mesquite Lime Seas Salt
2 tbs FreshJax Citrus Pepper Blend
1 cup Blue Cheese dressing

Directions
Pre heat sous vide bath to 185f/85c

Remove the core from the cabbage but do not go all the way through. Keep the large outside leaves for cover. Cut a small piece off the bottom of the cabbage to you can stand it up.

Mix the butter with half the seasonings and insert into the core of the cabbage. Take the outer leaves and cover the hole.

Vacuum seal in an expandable sealer bag and add to sous vide bath for 1 hour 20 minutes.

Pre-heat the smoker to 250f/121.11c

Mix the blue cheese dressing with the remaining seasoning.

Remove the cabbage from the bag and remove the outer leaves, add some of the blue cheese to the core and add the leaves back and place on the smoker for 20-30 minutes.

Remove from the smoker and chop into smaller pieces and place in a bowl and add the remaining dressing and toss.

Serve warm!

Sous-Vide RED MEAT ONLY Temp Chart

Chart created with the rule of 7. Rare is 122°F + 7°. Rule of 7 makes it easier to remember.

By Kevin Holmes Liddell

Rare	122–129°F
Medium Rare	130–137°F
Medium	138–145°F
Medium Well	146–153°F
Well Done	154°F ⇑

CHAPTER 10

REFERENCES AND RESOURCES

This section will give you many references to hopefully answer any questions you may have that were not answered in this book. The chart at the top of the page is a good example of that. Kevin Liddell over at the "Sous Vide Food and Fun" Facebook group has developed this chart with temperature ranges that are based on sous vide cooking temperatures alone. You can play with the temperatures within each range to figure your own sweet spot.

With red meat, important things to consider in selecting a doneness temperature is the fat you are looking to render and collagen to breakdown. Fat needs temperatures slightly higher than 131f/55c to start rendering, and collagen needs a lot of time to turn to gelatin at lower temperatures. The above guide gives you a basic range to work with on the "appearance" doneness only and not the overall doneness including tenderness.

Below you will find links to some other great sources you can bookmark and keep handy for future reference as you expand your knowledge of sous vide and barbecue.

Sous Vide and Barbecue Books and Guides

Of course, there are many other books out there that cover the many aspects of sous vide cooking in a lot more detail than this one. I did a lot of research and reading when I first discovered sous vide a few years ago and the books listed below helped me figure out the whys and what's but also gave me the confidence to experiment and create some new techniques. I highly recommend these books if you are looking to expand your knowledge of sous vide cooking.

- [Exploring Sous Vide by Jason Logsdon](#) Lots of great information and different recipes to help get you on the experimenting train. Jason also has several other sous vide books you can check out on amazon.
- [Under Pressure by Chef Thomas Keller](#) Chef Keller's book was one of the first that gave a comprehensive explanation of what sous vide is and could do in the professional kitchen. It can go over your head sometimes, but it does contain a ton of great information.
- [Sous Vide at Home by Lisa Fetterman](#) Lisa was one of the first people to help market a sous vide circulator aimed at the home cooks, the Nomiku. This book also has a lot of information great for a beginner.
- [Sous Vide for Everybody by America's Test Kitchen](#) Another great book for beginners that has a lot of information and recipes for you to try to learn sous vide.
- [Meathead: The Science of Great Barbecue and Grilling](#) the top selling barbecue and grilling book you will find anywhere! Meathead uses a scientific approach to explain why things work the way they do. One of my favorite overall cookbooks.
- [The Food Lab by J. Kenji Lopez-Alt](#) Another great science based cookbook that covers all kinds of foods and cooking methods. This will give you a great overall understanding of cooking in general.

Time and Temperature Guides – There are many different guides available and most sous vide circulators will come with a basic one to get you started. I have included a basic guide here, but there is also a list of a couple others that I use quite often and have found that the ranges they give are much more accurate than some others.

Fire & Water Cooking

Basic Time and Temperature Guide

This table is only meant to serve as a guideline. Temperatures listed are for medium doneness, adjust to your taste. Times denoted with an * include time for tenderness.

	Temp	Thickness	Time to Core Temp	**Time to Pasteurized**
BEEF				
Tenderloin	138°F / 59°C	2 inches	1 hour, 58 min	5 hours, 35 min
Rib Eye Steak	138°F / 59°C	1.5 inches	3 hours, 58 min	3 hours, 20 min
Strip Steak	138°F / 59°C	1.5 inches	2 hours, 58 min	3 hours, 20 min
Short Ribs	138°F / 59°C	2 inches	48 hours*	3 hours, 20 min
Brisket	147°F / 64°C		48 hours*	3 hours, 21 min
LAMB				9 hours, 03 min
Lamb Rack	138°F / 59°C	2.5 inches	3 hours, 16 min	3 hours, 51 min
Leg of Lamb	138°F / 56°C	4-5 inches	8 hours*	4 hours, 30 min
Lamb Shoulder	140°F / 60°C	3 inches	24 hours*	3 hours, 55 min
PORK				
Pork Chop	145°F / 63°C	1.75 inches	1 hour, 45 min	4 hours, 02 min
Ribs	140°F / 60°C		24-48 hours*	1 hour, 06 min
Shoulder/Butt	155°F / 68.33°C		36-48 hours*	8 hours
POULTRY				
Chicken Breast	145°F / 63°C	1 inch	1 hour 15 min	1 hour, 36 min
Duck Breast	135°F / 57°C	1 inch	60 min	2 hours, 41 min
Chicken Thighs	150°F / 65°C	1.5 inches	1 hours, 20 min	3 hours, 03 min
Turkey Breast	147°F / 64°C	5 inches	6 hours	6 hours, 20 min
FISH				
Salmon Filet	130°F / 54.4°C	1 inch	1 hour	5 hours, 09 min
Cod Filet	129°F / 54°C	1 inch	1 hour	3 hours, 47 min
SHELLFISH				
Shrimp / Prawns	135°F / 57°C	1 inch	30 min	5 hours, 21 min
Lobster	145°F / 63°C	1 inch	15 min	5 hours, 5 min
Scallops	135°F / 57°C	1.5 inches	1 hour	2 hours, 29 min
VEGETABLES				
Carrots	185°F / 85°C	1 inch	60 min	10 min
Potatoes	185°F / 85°C	3 inches	60 min	15 min
Cauliflower	185°F / 85°C	2 inches	1 hour	15 min

Amazing Food Made Easy - This is my favorite guide as it offers some really good ranges for doneness. https://www.amazingfoodmadeeasy.com/sous-vide-times-temperatures

Anova Culinary - Besides the guide they offer on their app for their circulator, Anova has an online version that was developed for them by J. Kenji Lopez-Alt. https://anovaculinary.com/anova-sous-vide-time-temperature-guide/

Sous Vide for the Home Cook - Douglas Baldwin took a couple years to put together this comprehensive guide to sous vide cooking and it offers up some great details on pasteurization times and temperatures based on the type of meat and the thickness. It is not the simplest read, but it has all the information you need for safe sous vide cooking. https://douglasbaldwin.com/sous-vide

ChefSteps Online Sous Vide Guide - ChefSteps was the creator of the Joule sous vide circulator before selling it off to Breville. They did create a great online guide to help you figure out sous vide times and temperatures and you can find it here. https://www.chefsteps.com/activities/sous-vide-time-and-temperature-guide

Sous Vide Tools - based in the UK, this online resource concentrates on selling commercial type sous vide equipment in Europe, but has a decent online sous vide time and temperature guide with the cut names most Europeans are familiar with like Topside, Blade of Beef, etc. https://us.sousvidetools.com/calculator

General Sous Vide and Barbecue Information-

Below are links to some very informational websites that offer up a little of everything. I did not invent sous vide barbecue, but I have been doing it and experimenting with it for a long time and I've focused a lot of my time and energy perfecting it. Below are some other great sites where you will find more information on using the methods together.

- **The Fire and Water Cooking Website** - For a lot of links and information on cooking with sous vide, barbecue, grilling, and smoking, check out my website. https://www.fireandwatercooking.com/

- **Amazing Ribs** - Besides all of the traditional outdoor cooking knowledge he has, Meathead Goldwyn saw early on the benefits that sous vide can bring to barbecue meats and he and his partner Clint Cantwell have some great information and recipes on the site. He also has a great deep dive sous vide que PDF book that is on amazon for just $3.99 that goes over some basics. There's some great articles on sous vide que and general meat science and barbecue that are good to know. This website is my "go to" for a lot of cooking knowledge. Look into joining the "Pitmaster Club" where you will have full access to all the information available by all of the many knowledgeable members as well.
https://amazingribs.com/bbq-technique-and-science
- **Amazing Food Made Easy** - Jason Logsdon has written several books on sous vide and other modernist cooking techniques and his website has tons of information including a free email sous vide course and a paid sous vide video course, tons of recipes, and time/temperature guide.
https://www.amazingfoodmadeeasy.com/
- **Serious Eats Sous Vide Cooking** - Serious Eats was one of the pioneers in bringing the sous vide cooking method to the home cook with lots of guides and recipes. J. Kenji Lopez-Alt did a lot of groundwork and experiments that show the best practices on using sous vide.
https://www.seriouseats.com/recipes/topics/method/sous-vide
- **CREA - Culinary Research & Education Academy**- Do you want to take an online video sous vide cooking class from the scientist who pioneered the process? For only $50 you can do just that! Check out this amazing course from the man who perfected it! http://www.lecrea.com/en/courses/online/
- **PolyScience Sous Vide Blog** - PolyScience was one of the first companies to help develop what were water bath circulators for laboratory experiments into devices that could be used in professional kitchens. Check out the great information in their blog that covers different aspects of sous vide and other precise temperature cooking.   https://polyscienceculinary.com/blogs/news
- **The Kosher Dosher Blog** - My friend Lloyd Cupiccia is just as crazy, if not more than I am about experimenting with sous vide cooking. He has done some amazing things and has perfected some of his own techniques with things like warm aging, sous vide ice cream, and much more!
https://kosherdosher.blogspot.com/p/sous-v.html

- **The International Sous Vide Association -** The International Sous Vide Association (ISVA) provides education, networking opportunities, and experiential events for enthusiasts (both professional and amateur) of the sous vide cooking method. The ISVA is an independent association (not directly affiliated with any particular brand or machine) focused on providing excellent information to the sous vide community. https://www.theisva.org/
- **Sous Vide Magazine** - This magazine is published by CREA and Cuisine Solutions, the inventors and refiners of sous vide cooking. It has some great information, recipes, and resources. https://www.sousvidemagazine.com/

Wrap up

I hope this book with its techniques, methods, and recipes has opened your eyes to how you can make some amazing food by combining sous vide and outdoor cooking. Once you start diving in, I know you will get the bug like I did. Be prepared to get involved in experiments and trying new things. Just remember to account for the longer cook times associated with some tougher meats and study the basics. Feel free to adjust the recipes to your tastes and make them your own.

Make sure you stay in touch with me through my social media outlets and follow my podcast at the links below.

Fire & Water Cooking Facebook Page - https://www.facebook.com/Fireandwatercooking

Fire & Water Cooking Facebook Group- https://www.facebook.com/groups/fireandwatercooking

Fire & Water Cooking YouTube Channel - https://www.youtube.com/c/FireWaterCooking

Fire & Water Cooking Instagram Feed - https://www.instagram.com/fireandwatercooking/

Fire & Water Cooking Podcast Audio Version - https://fireandwatercooking.buzzsprout.com/

RECIPE INDEX

Appetizers
Bacon wrapped moink balls, 50
Pork Belly Sliders, 55
Smoked Baby Back Ribs, 51
Smoked Brisket Burnt Ends, 53
Smoked Pig Wings, 52
Smoked Hot Chicken Wings, 54

Beef
Bacon Wrapped Meatloaf, 66
Big, Thick Medium Rare Burger, 59
Black Garlic & Coffee Rubbed Beef Ribs, 58
Coffee Rubbed NY Strip Steaks, 57
Pastrami Style Short Ribs, 63
Prime Rib, 67
Santa Maria Style Tri Tip, 65
Sous Vide Chuck Eye Steaks, 61
Sous Vide Beef Brisket, 64
Top Sirloin Steaks, 68
Tri Tip Surf and Turf, 60
Top Round aka London Broil, 62

Lamb
Greek Style Leg of lamb, 70
Lamb and Beef Kabob Gyros, 75
Lamb Spareribs, 71
Seared Lamb T-bones, 73
Smoked Lamb Shoulder, 74
Sous Vide Lamb Rack, 72

Pork
Barbecue Pulled Pork Shoulder, 82
Bacon Wrapped Pork Tenderloin, 77
Jamaican Jerk Pork Tenderloin, 81
Porchetta, 79
Pork Loin Roast, 83
Pulled Pork Carnitas, 78
St Louis Spareribs, 80
Thick Bone-in Pork Chops, 84

Poultry
Alabama Style Smoked Chicken, 91
Caribbean Jerk Chicken, 87
Cherry Wood Smoked Duck Fat Chicken, 86
Sous Vide and Smoked Whole Duck, 93
Smoked Fried Chicken, 90
Smoked Turkey Breast, 92
Spatchcocked Turkey, 89
Whole Rotisserie Chicken, 88

Seafood
Pineapple Habanero Bacon Shrimp, 99
Seared Sea Scallops, 98
Seared Tuna Steaks, 97
Seared Wild Cod, 95
Smoked Salmon Filets, 96

Vegetable Based Recipes
Black Bean Burger, 102
Grilled Cauliflower Steak, 103
Portobello Mushroom Steak, 104
Smoked Blue Cheese Slaw, 105
Tofu Barbecue Burnt Ends, 101

ABOUT THE AUTHOR

I fell in love with cooking at a young age. Watching my mother cook and bake everything from scratch in our home in upstate New York was the highlight of some of the cold long winters for sure. It was the warmest room in the house and the smells that wafted from there were intoxicating! She would show me how to make homemade meatloaf, whole chickens, lasagna, and many other wonderful dishes. One of my first jobs I had when I was in high school was washing dishes in a family diner, which led into a job as a short order cook when I turned eighteen.

I enjoyed my time working at different restaurants cooking different kinds and types of food, but the irregular hours and the low hourly pay was not something that lent itself to raising a family, so at the age of 23 I decided to go back to school and get into the banking business. That career has lasted over 30 years, but I never lost my love of cooking, and I continued to study and learn all kinds of cooking styles and methods and really fell in love with outdoor cooking. I am always the one cooking for the scout campouts, hosting the church potlucks, family reunions and any other get-together. Any chance I have to cook, I jump on it.

Fast Forward 2016, I was really big into cooking everything I could outdoors and was always trying new dishes and methods. I stumbled onto a YouTube video done by Greg Mrvich on his Ballistic BBQ YouTube channel that made me take notice. He was using this method called "Sous Vide" to cook a brisket and he was going to finish it on the smoker. I was totally enthralled and started down the path of total immersion (pun intended) of learning what sous vide was and what it could do when combined with smoking and grilling!

In 2017 I decided to start my own Facebook group dedicated to sous vide and barbecue, and then a couple months later I created a YouTube channel to do videos. After another six months I decided to give doing a podcast a try. The Fire & Water Cooking Brand Was Born! This book is another avenue in which I can help others learn what I have discovered to make awesome food.

I hope you learn something and spread the love of food with those around you! Make sure you check out Fire & Water Cooking on our website at www.fireandwatercooking.com, our Facebook page and groups, YouTube, Instagram, and subscribe to the Podcast and join the over 30,000 other followers!

www.ingramcontent.com/pod-product-compliance
Lightning Source LLC
Chambersburg PA
CBHW051257110526
44589CB00025B/2856